Escape from Catastrophe
1940 Dunkirk

Escape from Catastrophe
1940 Dunkirk

By
David J. Knowles

Published by
Knowles Publishing
Rochester

First Published 2000
Knowles Publishing, Rochester

ISBN 09534358 2 2

Front cover photograph –
Get on Anything that Floats!

Back cover photograph –
Heroes Return

Published by Knowles Publishing Rochester

Typeset by Academic & Technical Typesetting, Bristol
Printed by Redwood Books, Trowbridge, Wilts

Acknowledgments

My thanks to the following:

Ernie Leggett, editor of The Dunkirk Veterans Association Journal, for all his help, and letters sent out on my behalf.

The Imperial War Museum for pictures and information.

Mike Twyeman, Margate Historical Society. Bob Bradley at Margate Museum.

Michael Hunt at Ramsgate Maritime Museum. Tony Walters for information on lifeboats and for allowing me to use some lines from his book 'The Margate R.N.L.I. Station', Peter Barker coxswain Margate Lifeboat. Philip Atkins and The Railway Museum at York. Deal Maritime Museum. Brian Green and the Fishermens Museum at Hastings. Steve Peak for allowing me to use passages from his book, 'Fishermen of Hastings.' Mike Strong and Brighton Fishing Museum. John Iverson, Dover Museum. The London Weather Centre. B.B.C. Archives at Reading. Robert Chown for information on his grandmother – Florence Fullager.

James Tooley for information about the *Maid of Orleans* and for allowing me to use the account by the 2nd Engineer of the ship at the time of Dunkirk, his father George Tooley.

Noreen Chambers for information and pictures of *The Medway Queen*. John Puplett for information about the tug *Challenge*.

David Divine, for 'guidance' from his book – 'Dunkirk.'

John Richards and Sandy Evans for information on *Naiad Errant*. Trevor Harris, Steve Leach and Howard Smith Towage, Gravesend, for information on the 'Sun Tugs.' David Pament for information on *Ryegate II*. Steve Hastings for information on *Tigris I* the Thames pleasure boat that belonged to his grandfather, Harry Hastings at the time of Dunkirk.

Christian Brann for guidance and a line or two from his book 'The Little Ships of Dunkirk.' Larry Forrester for a few lines from his book 'Fly For Your Life.' Bob Tough, of Tough's Boatyard at Teddington for information about *Tigris I* as well as some facts about Tough's Boatyard at the time of Dunkirk – in particular about his father Douglas Tough. Harry Philcox, surviving member of the Shoreham Lifeboat, the *Rosa Woodd and Phyllis Lunn*. Captain James Brown(Trinity House Retired) for information about Deal boats. Simon Reid, information on Aldeburgh Lifeboat.

The reference libraries at Brighton, Chatham, Rochester, Chichester, Margate, Ramsgate and Sheerness. Isle of Thanet Gazette. Folkestone Express. Sheerness Times. Medway Today. Brighton Evening Argus. Dover Express. Folkestone Herald. Alan Readman, West Sussex Records Office, Chichester.

For all the following for writing to me about their time before and during the evacuation from the beaches of Dunkirk:

Albert Atkinson, Arthur Ayres, Albert Barnes, Don Booker, William Boultby, Bob Brooks, Frank Brookshaw, David Capel, Victor Chanter, James Cockfield, James Cowley, John Cranston, Jim Denne, Noel Eyley, Jack Farley, George Fox, Jim Hague, Gerald Johnson, Aubrey King, Vic Knight, Phyllis Knott, Norman Lees, Joe Lann, F.E. Lucas, John Mulloy, Joe Nixon, Philip Norburn, E. Oakland, Arthur Oates, Jim Peall, Bob Pendleton, Albert Powell, Norman Prior, Tommy Sands, Alan Scobie, Harry Stanley, D. Tait, Winifred Thorne, Dot Weedon, Tom Whelan, Ernie Wiggins, Bob Wrycraft, Arthur Young,

Also, Lt. Col. H.G.R. Boscawen for information about his nephew, Lt. Evelyn Boscawen.

Also my sincere thanks to anyone not mentioned here for their time and much appreciated help.

Contents

Illustrations

Escape from Catastrophe
1940 Dunkirk

Introduction

A few years ago, it was put to me by an elderly gentleman I know, (who had just read my book about a childhood in wartime Brighton, 'The Tree Climbers'), that I should write a book about Dunkirk – after first getting hold of as many accounts as possible from those who were there, and who might have hitherto untold stories to tell.

"It's about time someone did it   before it's too late!" He 'ominously' said to me. He knew that I have always had a special interest in this astonishing evacuation of an army.

I was just seven years of age at the time of Dunkirk, but I can remember that period of time quite well – mainly because of my father.

He was an ex army officer – a career man. He had been wounded at Mons in World War I, with the eventual loss of a leg. He felt frustrated, not only because of having a promising career cut short, but also because of not being a part of the action again; he had many friends who were in the British Expeditionary Force, and who he thought were probably in the thick of things, in France and Belgium.

When the news from Dunkirk started coming through, father keenly listened to all the wireless reports, as well as reading every paper he could lay his hands on, and was again frustrated by so many misleading articles and heavily censored reports.

At this time also, there was the very real fear of the home shores being invaded, and it didn't go unnoticed by my sister and myself that there was an air of tension – things weren't right!

After Dunkirk, attitudes changed, and despite all the fears, getting the troops back from Dunkirk had seemed like a victory on its own. I remember father saying, "They'll still be writing about Dunkirk in a hundred years from now – forever in fact!"

Heeding those words, and with encouragement from friends and relatives, and not being put off by so many other books being written on this subject – I decided to 'fire' ahead and write the book.

I have also heeded the advice my elderly friend gave me, and thanks to press coverages and help from associations such as, 'The Dunkirk Veterans Association,' I have put together a book which contains quite a few hitherto untold stories.

In the book, I have also included stories about the destroyers, the tugs, pleasure steamers, lifeboats, and of course, a variety of the 'little ships.'

There are also stories from those who were at the ports and railway stations to help the troops on their return.

On learning that I was definitely going to write the book, the elderly gentleman responsible for 'starting it all' said – "Now all you have to do is write it in time for the 60th anniversary of Dunkirk!"

That was 15 months ago – I now know the full meaning of the expression – "Time Flies!"

Chapter One

The Balloon Goes up – The retreat

My father's promising career as a regular army officer came to an abrupt end at Mons in the First World War. He escaped with his life, but the wounds he received were too bad for him to carry on as a professional soldier.

In 1937 the wounds in his left leg suddenly became gangrenous – he was rushed to hospital, and in a life saving operation the leg was amputated from well above the knee. This necessitated him putting his civilian job on the sidelines as well, and he settled down to a long period of recuperation.

In 1938, after the Munich agreement, many people thought there really would be 'peace in our time;' even father, who followed the news very closely, thought that it looked as though matters really had been settled.

During the early months of 1939, he changed his mind – "We're having the wool pulled over our eyes by Herr Hitler and his cronies!" I remember him saying to my mother.

At this time he still attended the army officer's hospital at Percival Terrace, near the seafront in Brighton. He went there to visit fellow officers, as well as for treatment on his leg. Their main topic of conversation was the ominous looking situation in Europe, and what part the army might be called upon to 'play' eventually.

When the 'balloon went up,' my father wasn't the only one amongst those in the main ward at the hospital who wished they could be part of the action again. It was frustrating for them, especially seeing that many of their friends and colleagues would be in the make up of the new British Expeditionary Force.

We lived in Sussex Square in Brighton – soon to become a restricted area because of it's coastal position. I was seven years of age at that time; my sister Jill was four years older than me – neither of us really took in a great deal of what was going on. We were aware, of course, that war had just been declared, and had sheltered in the basement of number thirteen when the first siren had blared out shortly after Mr. Chamberlain's announcement on that well remembered Sunday. Apart from this, I personally, whilst sometimes listening to some of the talk going on without understanding much of it, had more important things to do – such as playing with my friends in the spacious gardens that are entwined by Sussex Square and nearby crescents.

In the papers on September 4th 1939, we had been told what we should do in the event of air raids. Also, quite a bit had been written about evacuees and eventual evacuation of certain schools, about carrying gas masks wherever we went, and the fact that America was to remain neutral.

During the quiet months that followed the early panic – the time of little action the Americans dubbed "the phony war" – father still received letters from friends who were serving with the British Expeditionary Force in France. These letters told of some of what was going on in the army over there; but by the beginning of May the letters stopped. After this he had to rely on what the papers reported and what was said on the radio. At that time he was having difficulty in sleeping properly because of discomfort and pain in the stump of his left leg – had he had any idea of the huge drama that was about to unfold on the continent, he wouldn't have got any sleep at all. There was plenty of speculation of course, but also a lot of highly misleading articles in the papers. He felt frustrated, not only in not taking part in what was going on, but also in not knowing more of the situation – he wasn't alone in that respect.

The job that the B.E.F. was required to do, was to help to strengthen the French and eventually the Belgian armies against invasion by the Germans, who by early April had invaded Norway and were now concentrating on the low countries, including Holland.

Amongst the many regiments making up the British Expeditionary Force were – The Queen's Own Royal West Kents, The Royal East

14

Kents (The Buffs), The Royal Sussex Regiment, and many more from all over the UK including The Coldstream, Welsh and Grenadier Guards. The force was under the command of John Standish Prendergast Vereker – the 6th Viscount Gort. It was a surprise appointment; it had been thought that General Sir Edmund Ironside would get the job. General Gort, who most claimed to be 'a charming man given to schoolboyish enthusiasm,' didn't have the confidence of his two senior officers, who were – Lieutenant General Sir John Dill and Lieutenant General Brooke.

Advance parties of the B.E.F. had been taken across the channel as early as September 4th.1939 – both 1 and 2 corps were in France by October 1939.

The general opinion at that time of the British forces in France, was that the French army didn't seem too keen on going to war; their equipment was outdated and in any case they had had enough of fighting in World War I, which had ended just twenty one years beforehand. Also, they were confident that they had an impregnable defence of their borders in the Maginot Line. Soon after 1918 the construction of a huge defence rampart to keep the Germans at bay in the event of there being any more wars, was built to run from Basle to Longwy – where the French, Belgian and Luxembourg frontiers met. There was however a 'hole' in this defence network which ran along the Belgian border to Dunkirk – near the border in France. One of the plans for the B.E.F. was to help to defend this gap.

By the spring of 1940 the British Expeditionary Force had increased from 5 to 9 divisions, but many of the troops arriving to supplement the original force had hardly received any training before leaving England.

Eventually, the British were allotted a forty mile stretch of the French/Belgian border to defend. On arriving there, they were amazed to find that the only defences already there to hold any German attack, were a few pillboxes – manned by French soldiers equipped with 1914 rifles. They set about constructing a further 400 pillboxes on that section of the defence line – working sometimes in atrocious conditions, with poor rations. It became a time for 'using your loaf' – scrounging from where you could to make life a bit more bearable. It was quite a common sight to see men washing and

15

shaving in stream water. In the evenings, when they could get away, the men made a rush for the estaminets – fortunately the living was cheap there in those days.

David Caple of A Platoon 23, Coy. R.A.S.C. – part of General Montgomery's 3rd Ammunition Division, was luckier than most as far as food was concerned during the period of time before the Blitzkrieg. He and his Company had left Falmouth for Brest at the end of September 1939. At the beginning of their journey through France, they had travelled through the fruit growing areas, eating plenty of apples and pears on their way. Later, in Belgium, he had been in a convoy that had supplied the materials for building the pillboxes, but instead of having to 'scrounge' for his food, he had been befriended by a Belgian family who invited him to their home for meals each day. Although there were others who were lucky enough to receive similar hospitality, it was by no means a common occurrence. David's diet was to change considerably when the time came for retreating to the coast – but more about that later in the book.

On May 10th 1940, what up to then had been a relatively peaceful time for the B.E.F, suddenly changed to the harsh reality of all out war when the German 'Blitzkrieg' began. The French had thought that the densely forested area of the Ardennes was practically impassable for a large military force on the move – and consequently thought that only light protection was required there. This was a huge mistake – they had no idea of the might of General Guderian's Panzers, who eventually literally raced through the 'gap,' effectively cutting off the British and French troops who had been engaged elsewhere.

Earlier, on May 9th, General Erwin Rommel had written to his wife – "Dearest Lu, we're packing up at last, let's hope not in vain. You'll get all the news from the next few days from the papers. Don't worry yourself. Everything will go alright."

The next morning, Rommel's tanks crossed the southern end of the Belgian frontier – heading for the River Meuse at Dinant. At the same time, General Guderian, the spearhead commander, had made it quite clear to his senior officers that the eventual aim was the channel.

Rommel's wife probably got a true report on the situation from the German papers – there was no need for propaganda – the truth was amazing enough and almost beyond Hitler's wildest dreams that this position could have been gained so quickly.

Back at home, Mr. Chamberlain had at last resigned and Winston Churchill was now at the helm – just for a while the country paused to take a deep breath of relief – "The right man in the top job." My father echoed what most people were saying.

To make things seem somewhat rosier than they actually were, there were many optimistic reports in the papers. In The Times on Saturday May 11th, one article was headed – 'Belgians Confident of Victory – Ten times as strong as in 1914.' The article went on to say – 'The Belgian Ambassador in London, Baron de Cartier de Marchiere, in a broadcast from the BBC last night, said that his country's forces were ten times as great today as they were in 1914. Later in his speech he said – "Today, thanks to the wise leadership and foresight of King Leopold III, the keystone of whose policy has been to strengthen to the utmost the defences of the country, we face the aggressor with forces ten times as great, and we are fully confident that with the help of our old allies, we shall see the struggle through to victory."

By now, the British press were under strict censorship, with articles about the position on the continent, in some cases, highly misleading.

By May 16th, with Holland having capitulated the day before this, things were beginning to look even more grim, and the Germans, having already broken through at Sedan, had forced the allies to retreat from their critical positions on the Dyle and Meuse rivers – known as The Dyle/Meuse Line.

Back in April – on April 9th, the Germans had invaded Norway and Denmark. The British had sent troops to help Norway on April 15th – on May 2nd they withdrew. Because of this news, at home, the speculation amongst the discerning had increased to be more than just passing remarks, and it was hardly surprising that people with 'military minds' – such as my father – were extremely sceptical of what they were being told the position was with the B.E.F.

When the British troops withdrew from Norway on May 2nd, the position in Europe looked extremely ominous, but the reports of what the future might hold at that time, had none the less been smothered with misleading optimism – the muddle was beginning.

17

Later in the month, on the 17th May, the Belgian government moved to Ostend, but there were still quite a few days to go before it would become anything like clear to the British public just how serious the whole situation was. However, also on the 17th May, the government secretly started to prepare for mass evacuations from the coastal areas where the invasion was most likely to take place.

At number thirteen Sussex Square, my grandparents had already decided to leave the house in my parents charge – they had moved to Cumberland, "– until things across the water look a bit healthier." Grandfather said.

It was my parents custom, as indeed it was by just about the whole of the country during the war years, to make a point of listening to the news bulletins on the radio – particularly the ones at nine o'clock in the evenings. Even we children listened in eagerly now – not so much for hearing the news, but to hear if Bruce Belfrage was reading it; he and his wife and son Julian had recently moved into the top flat at number 13, and Julian had joined our set of friends. My father, quickly struck up a friendship with this well known news reader, and often tried to glean from him – "what was going on behind the scenes." This was mainly without success, because even those at the BBC weren't by any means in possession of much more knowledge of the state of things on the continent than the rest of the public. He did confirm however, to father, that he thought things were considerably worse than was being reported. One particular thing I remember about Bruce Belfrage living in the same house as us, was that later on when the bombing had started, it seemed strange to have listened to him reading the nine o'clock news to the nation, and few hours later find him sheltering with us, during a night air raid, in the basement at no. 13.

Back on May 15th, in France, when things were looking disastrous practically everywhere for the French army and the allies, General Gamelin, the officer commanding the French forces at that time, was still confident that the tide would turn. However, late in the evening of that day, when the French received the news that German tanks had reached Montcornet, and at the same time got word that the roads were choked with routed French troops, Gamelin, who up to then had been saying that the 'gaps' in the defence could soon be

18

patched up, seemed at long last to grasp the real situation and realised it could mean the destruction of the French army.

That night, the French government decided to appeal to Mr. Churchill – asking for more support from the air, and General Gamelin ordered the withdrawal of French troops from Belgium. Also at this time, Paul Reynaud, the French premier, gave the order for the government to prepare to move to Tours, and he wired to Churchill: "Last evening we lost the battle – the way to Paris lies open. Send all the troops and planes you can!"

On May 17th, the Panzers reached the Sambre – Oise canal at Laon; not much more than sixty miles from Paris. On the same day the allied retreat from Belgium had begun – not helped in any way by the increasing activities of the Luftwaffe.

On May 18th, the Germans, led by their supreme tactician, General Guderian, captured St. Quentin and Peronne. The day after this, Reynaud called in Petain as deputy premier and appointed General Weygand, at 73 years of age, to take over the command of the French forces from a highly disillusioned General Gamelin.

By May 20th, Hitler was said to be – 'Beside himself with joy!' He had been told that the Panzers were within sight of the channel and effectively cutting off the B.E.F.'s retreat routes.

The General headquarters of the British Expeditionary Force had been at the town of Arras since it's arrival in France. In the First World War, in 1914, the town had been entered by the Germans. In 1917 there was a huge battle here, quite simply called 'The Battle of Arras.' There was another great German attack here in March 1918, but the French held on to the town, and in the September of that year, the allies drove the enemy away. A war memorial was placed here in 1932.

Arras stands on the Scarpe river and is 28 miles from Amiens. It is a market town, and although now famous for the battles fought there, it is also renowned for tapestry making. Now Arras found itself once again the focal point for the Germans, and amongst those of the B.E.F. who were to help defend here and lend support to the crack Welsh Guards, were the 12th. 23rd. and 46th divisions – it was hoped that this force could hold the Panzers. A lot of these reinforcements were hardly trained and the equipment they possessed was minimal.

It was at this time that Major General Richard Petre, a very experienced and competent officer, was put in charge of this force – it became known as 'Petre force.' However, he faced a seemingly impossible task; not only had many of the troops not even completed basic training, but they were also inexperienced in the use of weapons such as the Bren-guns that they were supposed to be effectively using. The fighting soon became very fierce, but also unfortunately, things started to become somewhat chaotic. Also making up 'Petre force' were the 6th and 7th Battalions, The Queens own Royal West Kents and the 5th Battalion The Royal East Kent Regiment (The Buffs); with all of these taking part in the action, but spread over a wide area – there was some confusion. Jim Peall, a corporal in The Buffs at that time, related the following to me:

"On the 19th April 1940, the Battalion left Southampton for LeHavre. From there we travelled to a small town in Normandy called Fleury – Sur – Andelle, quite close to Rouen. C company ended up being housed in an empty warehouse, surrounded by lakes and streams. I should make it quite clear here that the whole time I was in France, I never knew where I was, where I was going or what I was doing – hardly anybody did! Apparently, the top brass wanted it kept that way. My days seemed to be filled with route marching and teaching the Bren-gun – of which I knew absolutely nothing! We were eventually marched off from this place in full pack, with my section, as usual, selected to be the scouting section ahead of the battalion. We were supposed to be looking out for parachutists, but I was more preoccupied in wondering where we were supposed to be going. We eventually found ourselves under canvas at a place called Poix.

Whilst we were at this place I noticed that the road that ran between our camp and our work site, was packed with refugees. Before long we were on the move again, this time ending up at Doullens, and after spending the evening visiting the estaminets here, we slept in an empty convent. The next morning my section was told to convert a very nice looking detached house, facing a beautiful tree lined stream, into a stronghold and defend it to the last man. This would have been alright if some of the more 'adventurous' of my section hadn't discovered that the house had an extensive wine cellar

– still well stocked up! I believe that some kind French neighbour had tipped our lads off. Needless to say it wasn't too long before we all took advantage of this unexpected new source of refreshment.

The next few hours could be described as a 'break from the monotony of things' – or a thoroughly enjoyable impromptu party!

It was unfortunate that just as all the hilarity and singing were in full swing, that our company commander, Captain Hilton, decided to inspect our position. I had reckoned that should there be an attack by the Germans, my lads would have sobered up quickly enough; I had also reckoned that if we met up with any crack German regiments – with our amount of training in battle techniques – we wouldn't have stood a chance in any case.

Captain Hilton was not at all amused at being confronted by such goings on, and had it not been for being captured soon afterwards – my stripes might have been in danger!

The next morning, we all piled into lorries and were driven through roads filled with refugees.

Later, we found ourselves on the road to Arras – which we were given orders to defend. Eventually, after vainly trying to stop an attack of innumerable German tanks with our sparse selection of weapons, I led what was left of my section away from this hopeless situation. We crossed over fields, climbed along ditches and behind hedges, until eventually, totally exhausted, we crept into a small wood to sleep for the rest of the day. I fell into a deep sleep and was awakened by a lot of shouting – not in English! I found myself at the wrong end of a rifle. I spent the next five years as a prisoner of war."

By this time, there was fierce fighting going on in many areas in that part of eastern France, and to write about everything that was going on would fill several volumes, but one particular action I must mention here, took place quite near to Amiens. The following, is an account of that action printed in The Times on the last day of 1943:

On May 18th 1940, the 7th Royal Sussex entrained for Lens, and just outside Amiens became the target for a heavy bombing attack. In all some 100 of the 500 members of the Regiment on the train were casualties. The survivors were doubled into a small wood less than half a mile away from the railway, and there reorganised. It was not a peaceful night that they spent in the wood, for they were repeatedly bombed, and even in the intervals, many delayed action bombs shattered the silence.

On the following morning the Battalion left the wood and was re-positioned on the neighbouring high ground for dispersal rather than defence, for there was no idea of occupying a tactical position. By now the bombing of Amiens had begun in earnest, and the German aircraft paid particular attention to the wood in which the Royal Sussex had recently been sheltering. During the afternoon refugees in an unbroken stream poured down the road to Poix. By the afternoon of May 20th several reports had been received that the Germans were in Amiens in force. The stream of refugees was now but a thin trickle, and it was clear that the Royal Sussex were left without the support of the allied troops who had been in the vicinity. They stood alone in the face of the German advance.

The commanding officer called his company commanders together and explained that, as he had received no orders it was his intention to hold the high ground to the last. The battalion, on a front about 440 yards long, was drawn before the Amiens-Rouen Road. Early in the afternoon the enemy made contact, and mortar and shell fire soon developed. Shortly after 3 o'clock an enemy attack was launched against the battalion's centre, and soon it was decided to attempt to relieve pressure there and drive the enemy back by advancing one reserve company and the company on the right of our line, while relying on the remaining reserve company to conform from the right flank. Within a few minutes the battle developed and continued for some hours.

The Royal Sussex fought with dogged valour and refused to yield ground. The companies which had come to the relief of the centre of the line, in spite of the heavy odds against them, refused to capitulate until late in the afternoon, when they were virtually overwhelmed by the enemy tanks. At 5.30 the commanding officer, who had been making a tour of the battalion's positions, met on the right of the battalion's front, a group of 20 men who reported numbers of enemy tanks. He organised them into two sections, and led them on to the high ground, and himself went forward to try to ascertain the situation. He had almost reached the crest when he found himself faced by several enemy tanks, which suddenly appeared on the right. These, though not until an hour later, forced him to surrender.

The gallant resistance had been an amazingly successful bluff. It was certain that a force which amounted to little more than half the strength of a full battalion, could not, more than momentarily, hold the high ground against a Panzer division with any real prospect of success. As the commanding officer himself observed, if the Germans had known the real situation, they could have cleared the positions in five minutes. In fact however, the desperate and unflinching defence offered by the battalion succeeded in delaying the enemy's advance for at least six hours, and that meant until the next morning. The Royal Sussex had given splendid effect to those instructions given by the commanding officer to his company commanders: "Our original orders were to proceed to Lens. That is impossible. We have no orders to go back. Therefore we stay where we are."

It remains to add that the Panzer division which encountered this small force of British troops was commanded by no less a leader than General Rommel. During a parade at Oflag IX A/H Spangenburg, Germany, Oberleutnant Richter, who was with General Rommel's division, recognized the commanding officer of the 7th. Royal Sussex, and admitted to him that the German formation had travelled 70 kilometres since dawn on May 20th, and that this had been the first serious resistance they had met. He added, that because of the gallantry shown by this tiny force , his division was checked in its advance until daylight on May 21st. Rommel himself was admitted to be personally in command of the operation, and the commanding officer of the Royal Sussex was in fact handed over to him on being taken prisoner.

In The Daily Mirror, on May 21st, an article was headed – 'The French Drive Nazis Back.' In actual fact, the French were preparing a counter offensive on Arras for the 23rd. May – but the British had gone ahead and launched their own attack at the same time as the Mirror readers were digesting what the paper said the French had already done – in other words the counter attack by the British was on the 21st May. General Gort had used his 5th and 50th divisions and his armoured brigade, which were somewhat depleted by then. This was under the command of General Franklyn, who was hoping to link up with the new French 3rd. army group, which was preparing to attack from a westerly direction on the 23rd May. The actual attack by the British, which began at 14.00 hours on the 21st was only on a small scale – Nevertheless, it came as quite a shock to Rommel's Division by gaining 16 kilometers and destroying a large number of enemy tanks. The surprise had been such that Rommel signalled that evening – "Very heavy fighting took place between 15.00 and 19.00 hours, with hundreds of enemy tanks and their supporting infantry." General Von Rundstedt was later to say that the Arras attack was the only allied offensive which inspired any fear in him in May 1940, and certainly the Elan of the Panzer force had been badly shaken. They made no more mass attacks after this date and it seemed that this action helped in the eventual success at Dunkirk.

In The Times on May 21st. a report by their special correspondent said – 'The German push was pressed forward with great violence in both Belgium and France at the weekend.'

By now things were getting rather confusing, with some papers 'hedging their bets' by even publishing two contrasting reports on the same page! One report that was correct, but still confusing, appeared in the same paper the following day, it said '– Monsieur Reynaud, the prime minister of France, spoke out with great frankness to the French senate yesterday (says Reuter) about the serious position in which France and her allies find themselves. He stated that Arras and Amiens were occupied by the Germans yesterday morning. He went on to say – "The country is in danger. My first duty is to tell the truth to the senate and the country."

On reading these pieces of news, my father could hardly contain himself; he had an appointment at the Army Officers Hospital that day, and he was eager to hear what everybody there made of the reports and the present situation.

I remember that it was at that time that I overheard a conversation which was mainly about my uncle Jimmy – my mother's brother. He

24

was with the B.E.F. and there had been no letters from him for over four weeks. Understandably, mother was very worried about him – as were we all. He was my favourite uncle – more importantly, he actually drove a tank. I also remember that I wasn't exactly 'backward in coming forward' about this piece of information to all my friends!

With the B.E.F. on the retreat and the position on the continent looking grim, there was a lot of talk about evacuating schools. My sister was attending St. Mary's Hall school for girls in Kemptown, Brighton. I was also attending the kindergarten there, before going on to Brighton College Preparatory School. St. Mary's Hall was very close to us – with a part of it actually in Sussex Square. Our parents were very worried about the situation, and with the probability of the home shores being invaded, there had been some talk of going to stay on a relative's farm in Surrey, but with the new restrictions on travel and leaving the town, this was now very difficult – if not impossible to do.

The situation regarding our defences, should the invasion come, looked very bleak and I remember Father commented, "It's all very well sending all those troops to France and Belgium, but right now they're needed back here – desperately! The sooner Mr. Churchill sees fit to get them back, the better!"

On the 19th May a letter had arrived at number thirteen and many other addresses, from the headmistress of St Mary's Hall – Miss. E. Stopford, saying that they believed, after reassurances from the A.R.P. (Air Raid Precaution) authorities, that the school could carry on as it was; after all, it had been pointed out that the evacuation would be rather futile as the west country and the north would be just as exposed to attack as the south east!

This, at least temporarily solved the problem, but I can remember my mother saying – "we are at the stage when we have no idea how different things will be on every tomorrow!"

Back on the continent, after Arras and further German advances, General Brooke had entered in his diary on May 23rd – "Nothing but a miracle can save the B.E.F. now, and the end cannot be far off."

By the 25th May, General Gort had decided to occupy a barrier position along the canal from Comines to Ypres. In the meantime King Leopold had issued a 'Proclamation Pathetique' to his troops – "The great battle which we feared has begun. It will be hard. We shall fight with all our strength and with supreme courage. We shall struggle on this soil where we victoriously halted the invader in 1914. Belgium expects you to honour the flag. Soldiers, whatever the outcome, my fate is with you."

After further German advances, King Leopold sent General Blanchard the following message:

'The Belgian command requests you to inform the commander in chief of the allied armies, that the situation of the Belgian army is grave and the Belgian command intends to continue the fight to the very end. Nevertheless, the limits of resistance have now practically been reached!'

Before this, on May 23rd, for some still unknown reason, the main German advance came to a halt, giving the retreating B.E.F. and French troops a breathing space – a lifesaving gift!

The opportunity that the Germans had at that time of finishing off the British and French troops, was thrown away as the Panzers were ordered to pull back across the Aa river. Although the original order came from Hitler and was passed on by Von Rundstedt, it was maintained later by the Fuhrer's chief of staff, Keitel, that he was unjustly credited with the responsibility of making the wrong decision. Whoever was responsible – the only reasonable explanations to this happening, are that it was thought by some in the German high command, that they were advancing so swiftly that they could very well be heading into a trap and they needed time to appraise the situation, or that after two weeks non stop attack, time was needed for repairs and rest – perhaps both. Also, the reputation of the British at war, and the counter attack by the B.E.F. at Arras, might have helped to make the Germans cautious. Whatever the answer – as one senior B.E.F. officer said – "The pause was heaven sent!"

Back in England, with the outlook everywhere looking grim, King George VI, speaking on Empire Day to the nation on the radio, called for the following Sunday to be a day of national prayer. "Make no mistake, it is no mere territorial conquest that the enemies are seeking." He said in that broadcast. "It is the overthrow – complete and final – of this Empire and of everything for which it stands, and after that the conquest of the world."

On the 26th May, Anthony Eden, secretary of state for war, sent General Gort a telegram in which he said that if the information he had received was true – as far as the plight of the B.E.F. was concerned – the only course open to you may be to fight your way back to the west where all the beaches and ports east of Gravelines will be used for embarkation. At this time also, Churchill contacted Vice-Admiral Ramsay at Dover and ordered that 'Operation Dynamo' be put into effect forthwith!

About that morning, Churchill, in his memoirs, recalled the 'pent up passion' of the people attending the service at Westminster Abbey. At home, mother and father attended the service at St. Mark's church, nearby – father didn't usually attend, but mother was a regular churchgoer; she later told us that the church was packed. I remember that I noticed that father was unusually quiet, and that mother was white faced, tight lipped and drawn. One thing I remember father saying to a friend who called in for a chat, was that he wondered whether the children would be sent away from the town in the event of an invasion. Brighton, as indeed many coastal towns in eastern, south eastern and southern England, would probably be in the front line of the fighting when the invasion came. I remember that he said those last words as though it 'would' happen. He also talked about what a difference it would make to get all or most of the troops of the B.E.F. back home – "Then we'd stand a good fighting chance!" He said.

Back on the 22nd May on the roads and lanes of Belgium and France, over fields and through streams, rivers, woodlands and canals, the British Expeditionary Force, now almost in total disarray, had desperately started to head for the French port of Dunkirk. Many rearguard actions were being fought at this time, and with Calais seemingly soon to fall, the plan was to tighten the perimeter of defence around Dunkirk in a narrow semi circle, extending from Nieuport in the east, to Gravelines, near Calais, in the west. It had therefore been essential to hold on to Calais for as long as possible. Accordingly, on the 22nd./23rd of May, special forces had been

27

put ashore at Calais under the command of Brigadier Claude Nicholson. At the least, Nicholson's orders were to 'buy' precious time – but sounding more sinister – to fight to the last man!

I feel that before telling the story of Dunkirk, I should tell of the brave defence of Calais.

Chapter Two

Defence of Calais

The small British force that was landed at Calais under the command of Brigadier Claude Nicholson was, amongst other things, there to keep communications open with Dunkirk including opening new supply lines to the troops there. In what became a muddled operation, Nicholson was ordered to go to Boulogne and help defend there. This order was quickly cancelled and he was then ordered to stay where he was and – "Defend Calais to the last."

A born optimist, Nicholson, none the less knew that he had a seemingly impossible task in successfully defending the port for very long, however, he was determined to – "Make a damn good go of things!"

They had arrived on 22/23rd May to supplement the force already there. Amongst the troops sent, were The 3rd Royal Tank Regiment and The Queen Victoria Rifles – these had arrived on the 22nd of May They were followed on the 23rd by two Battalions of regulars, including the 2nd Battalion, The Kings Royal Rifle Corps (60th Rifles) and the 1st. Battalion, The Rifle Brigade – all these immediately came under Nicholson's command.

By mid-day on Thursday 23rd. May, the usually busy harbour at Calais lay deserted except for the ships coming to take away the wounded and the 'useless mouths.' Most of the small boats usually to be found there had 'disappeared' – it was a sinister scene.

Calais was crowded with people trying to escape the city – there were also people trying to get into the city, hopefully to escape by boat – it was a scene of general confusion!

With the fall of Boulogne imminent, Calais was now the focal point for the Germans in their pincer movements from the west to trap the greater part of the British Expeditionary Force. Further to the west, Cherbourg, and other places wouldn't be attacked until after the evacuation of 'Dunkirk' – Paris wouldn't fall until June 14th.

The 'useless mouths' that were being sent back, were the ones doing clerical duties and the like. It seems odd that they could, so recently, have been sending troops to the continent with such little training and who were now in the thick of the fighting, when they were probably less trained than the 'useless mouths' they were now sending home from Calais.

Also arriving in Calais – not from the sea but overland, were the remnants of units, scattered in various skirmishes and now seeking some definite guidance – these too quickly came under the command of Brigadier Nicholson. At this time also, the Germans increased in momentum their shelling of the harbour. This made everything very difficult, to say the least, – particularly for the ships coming in to take people off, including the wounded – two trains full of wounded men had arrived in Calais that day, 23rd May.

The wounded in these trains had seen fighting in many different places, but were mainly from areas well to the east – many of them had been three days on their journey. It became necessary to use some of the fighting troops in Calais to carry many of these wounded men onto the ships that would take them home – some had already died on the journey. One of the wounded was Joe Nixon of the 2nd Battalion, The Coldstream Guards – 1st Brigade. To enlighten the reader of how he came to be there, this is Joe's story – as he related it to me.

Joe had been put aboard a train with other wounded at Pecq near the French/Belgian border – not far from Lille. He says:

"By May 10th, we were carrying out a series of rear guard actions. One of my indelible memories is of marching along a main road that brought us to a cross roads which had been pinpointed by German artillery – it was somewhere near here that while on a two man 'recce' of our defences on our side of the Escaut river, with Lt. Boscawen of the Falmouth family (Lord Falmouth), that we discovered a five hundred yards gap. Now don't forget that for every position we had to defend, we were armed with just Bren-Guns and rifles – and this was against the might of the German tanks and artillery – it was hopeless really. The Germans even thought that we considered our Bren-Gun carriers were tanks! In any case, enemy activity was very evident right up to the opposite bank of the river, so a recce patrol was very much needed, especially to make contact with the adjoining Grenadier Guards. It was night time and my officer and I did this patrol in pitch darkness. We carefully counted our steps – it was very tense and eerie. I could hear splashes coming from the other bank and have no doubt that the Germans were undertaking their own 'recce'. After about 500 yards, we were challenged by a Grenadier sentry, which would have been on their number 4 company's extreme left flank. Although we were very edgy, the lieutenant and I safely passed this platoon position. We went on to see the company commander, Major West, again being challenged strongly by another Grenadier century.

Lt. Boscawen gave his report of the very vulnerable gap existing between our company and the Grenadiers, and it was quickly agreed with Major West that we would return immediately to extract the centre platoon of our company and place it in a position to cover the gap; Lt. Boscawen and I then quickly paced back, as near as possible, to the halfway mark. The lieutenant stayed some distance back from our side of the river bank to receive the platoon. I hurried back to number one company's front position on the Escaut bank, to request that number eight platoon pull out and accompany me back to the lieutenant's position. I guided this platoon back to my officer. He then instructed me to return with all speed to number 1 company H.Q., situated on higher ground some distance back from the platoon positions, and advised the company commander of the gap and the emergency action taken. I carried out these instructions, but although very willing to return to Lt. Boscawen, I was then ordered by the company commander to man a trench, as manpower was very low. Sadly, about half an hour later – it was still pitch black don't forget – a Coldstream sentry challenged a figure looming out of the darkness and, not receiving the correct response fired and fatally wounded Lt. Boscawen.

When I eventually found out about this tragedy, I crawled over to where he lay to retrieve his Coldstream Star cap badge, which I had previously put into his small pack when we had exchanged caps for steel helmets. As his runner in action, we had made a mutual agreement on this – should either of us be killed. I put this star in my trousers pocket, and for the time being, with all that was going on, forgot about it.

Somewhat later, whilst we were desperately defending a position near a canal bank – our 303 rifles against the might of the enemy – reinforcements arrived in the shape of four Bren-Gun carriers, which charged along the road towards us. The Germans opened fire – scoring a direct hit on Captain Fane's carrier. He was hit in the head and killed; the same shell also wounded Guardsman Sanderson and myself. Someone put a field dressing on me, then I hobbled off towards the casualty clearing station at Pecq. There, I found the Royal Army Medical Corps people to be real experts – extremely professional. I was eventually put on a hospital train with many other wounded troops – after several days we arrived at Calais. I remember some troops helping me and the others on board a ship – I remember they were very considerate and caring. It wasn't until I was having my trousers taken away from me back in England that a nurse discovered Lt. Boscawen's badge in my pocket." There is more of Joe Nixon and Lt. Boscawen in the epilogue.

Amongst the men who were defending Calais, and who had been told to help to carry some of the wounded to a ship, was Vic Knight – a regular soldier of the 1st Battalion The Rifle Brigade – Vic had joined the army in 1938. He told me – "The battalion arrived in Calais on May 23rd, by when, evacuation from there was already underway. As the vehicles came ashore, they were filled with men and driven off immediately to the positions they were required to defend. There was no time in between – it was off the ship and straight to it! I remember that there were some non-combatants getting ready to board a ship for back home, and we took the ammunition that they had, off them – our need was greater than theirs! Our lot didn't have any vehicles though, there had been some big mix up there, so all those of us without vehicles were formed into a 'scratch' company. This was done at the quayside, and while we were there, two hospital

32

trains arrived. I was one of the ones who went to help carry the wounded to the ship. In later years I got to know Joe Nixon through the Dunkirk Veterans Association, but he could well have been one of the ones I helped to carry to the hospital ship. I can't remember the name of the ship we carried the wounded to, but I do remember that before leaving Calais for England, the captain of the ship threw some packets of cigarettes down to us, and wished us – "Good luck!"

After this, I remember there was a lot of fighting, and the ammunition was low. We didn't seem to take much notice of time just when it was light or when it was dark. Towards the end, I remember diving under cover into a sort of tunnel when the shelling seemed to be nonstop. I remember also seeing a few of the officers at this time, including Lt. Tony Rolt. There was a first aid post here as well. For much of this time we were under continuous attack from Stukas. Some time later, after a lot of fighting, I eventually took up a position on a beach – I think this was an area they call The Dunes. By this time I was exhausted and I remember I went to sleep on this beach. When I woke up I saw there were some Germans approaching – I only had a couple of rounds left, so resistance would have been useless. I buried the Bren-Gun breech block in the sand – others near to me buried their rifle bolts, so the German couldn't make use of our guns. The Germans came over to me and said – "Hands hoch" – or something like that; in any case I put my hands up, and all of a sudden I was a prisoner. I remember I dropped my cigarettes, but they allowed me to pick them up and keep them. After this we were marched back into the centre of Calais, where there were several others that I knew amongst the captured. The next morning we started on the long march to our first prisoner of war camp – I remember we marched into the camp at attention, just to show them that despite how ragged and worn out we looked, we were still part of the British Army." Vic spent five years as a prisoner of war. I have included another piece about him in the epilogue.

To give a clearer picture of what was being defended, I will put in here the following description of Calais, which was included in some facts sent to me from the Headquarters of The Royal Green Jackets in Winchester:

33

'Calais, with a population in 1939 of 60,000–70,000 inhabitants, fell into two distinct parts. The old town, with its narrow, irregular streets, was bounded on the north east by the harbour, and on the west by The Citadel with its 17th century fort and moat. The new town, built on more regular, modern lines, lay to the south and south east; the whole, being surrounded by a rampart and moat enclosing a rough square, some 3,000 yards across. The old town was enclosed by the 'Bassin Carnot' (an extension of the harbour) on the east, and by the Bassin de Batallerie on the south. Between the harbour and the Bassin Carnot, two swing bridges gave access to the old town from the Gare Maritime.'

The weather in Calais was hot – almost sultry. Through the bombings, the water mains had been hit, and there was little drinking water. Despite the 'siege' situation, there was still the occasional estaminet to be found open, so wine was also obtainable. One soldier, a couple of days later, came across one of these 'pubs' – now deserted, but with some of the stock still on the premises – he helped himself! He was in considerable pain from a wounded knee and foot. He made himself as comfortable as possible in a 'sniping position' in a deserted house; he was armed with – "a fair amount of ammo, four bottles of plonk and plenty of fags – I quite enjoyed myself." He said. Later, he was taken prisoner – but can't remember much about it!

At this time, with the British defending Calais 'to the last man' – the French troops there seemed to be in two minds; there were some who didn't want any more fighting, and quite simply didn't bother any more, and others who defended and fought with amazing courage and dedication. On the 25th May, Brigadier Nicholson established his headquarters in The Citadel. He had lost all communication with London by this time – but he was still in touch with Dover. His request for more air support didn't get the response he had hoped for, however, two destroyers off shore – *The Verity* and *The Windsor* continued to engage the German batteries.

By late in the afternoon of Saturday the 25th May, the men of The Rifle Brigade were on the dunes – trying to defend various positions, but there was some general confusion here as well. There were refugees going to and fro all over the place, and some of the men had

34

now become cut off from Calais. During this time there was still a heavy bombardment going on – this lessened a bit that night. Just before midnight, Nicholson received the following message from Churchill or, someone in the government under Churchill's instructions – "Every hour you continue to exist is of the greatest help to the B.E.F. The government has therefore decided you must continue to fight. Have greatest possible admiration for your splendid stand."

On that fateful day – the 25th May, the casualties had been very heavy. At one time, Nicholson had been reported – "killed in the bombardment of The Citadel." This, of course, was incorrect – later on he was to congratulate the Rifle Brigade on their action that day. He still emphasised that Calais was to be held to the last – no evacuation!

The chief difficulty in organising the defence of the houses, was that most of them could only be entered from the front doors, in full view of the enemy; so holes had to be broken through side and back walls. Windows were smashed to eliminate danger from flying glass, and locked doors burst open. A great many civilians were removed from the houses in the front line, but the Battalion area was full of those who hid. There were well over 1,000 French and Belgian soldiers – now demoralised and unarmed. All this led to many 'fifth columnist' scares – there were certainly some snipers behind the lines. A sniper, with a sub machine gun, was supposed to be in the roof of the cathedral.

During that very warm night there were heavy bombardments by the Luftwaffe. One vivid description of how Calais looked that night was made by 2nd Lt. Jabeth-Smith. His account also appears in Airey Neave's memorable book, 'The Flames of Calais,' the Lieutenant said:

"It was a very clear, warm night. At sea were the dark forms of the warships, and the sky in their direction was crossed and recrossed with the beams of hundreds of searchlights from the English coast and from the ships. – Calais was on fire – red, orange and yellow flames burned skywards from various points in the town. Between us and the city was a lake called 'The Bassin des Channes,' and in this the flames were reflected. The scene made me think I was witnessing the sacking of some Medieval city."

When dawn broke on the 26th May – with the ships clearly visible at sea it was hoped that they might send their lifeboats, but these ships soon came under heavy shelling themselves, making this impossible.

At just after 8 a.m. and under a flag of truce, the Germans demanded that Nicholson and what remained of his scattered force – "surrender!"

Nicholson was in no doubt, there was no hesitation in his answer – "No" – he said.

During that last fateful day, Lt. Tony Rolt – whom Vic Knight had noticed just before making his final stand on the sand dunes – with about twenty men of The Rifle Brigade and Queens Volunteer Rifles, made one last attempt at trying to hold an important line near a tunnel on the road to Bastion de L'estran – but the Germans were there before them. Rolt and some of the men rushed at them – most of them were killed. Rolt, who had already won the Military Cross for his part in the fighting in Calais, had performed his last act of defiance – the battle lost, he surrendered his two empty revolvers.

The Battle for Calais was over – for four days these brave men had fought so that others might get away. They had bought with their lives and their freedom, the most valuable time imaginable.

Later, Churchill, when asked about the giving of the order – "To the last man" – said "I gave that order; it was my decision, although it sickened me to have to do it. But it was Calais that made the evacuation of Dunkirk possible."

To the east, at Dunkirk, the huge drama there was beginning to unfold, and at Dover, a man whom destiny had perhaps chosen to be at the right place at the right time, was about to organise the greatest mass rescue of all time.

Chapter Three

Operation Dynamo – The evacuation begins

On Sunday May 26th 1940, the day that King George VI had asked to be a national day of prayer, Vice Admiral Bertram Ramsay, at Dover, was given the order that 'Operation Dynamo,' the evacuation of Dunkirk, was to go ahead forthwith.

Ramsay, born at Hampton Court in 1883, had distinguished himself well during World War I. He had been two years on the Dover Patrol and in 1918 was mentioned in dispatches by Sir Roger Keyes, Vice Admiral Dover at that time.

In 1935, Ramsay became chief of staff to the Commander-in-Chief of the home fleet. Things were going well and it looked as though he was heading for the pinnacle of success in his chosen career. This was not to be – he soon discovered that in his job, he and his staff had practically nothing to do. The Commander-in-Chief of the home fleet, Admiral Sir Roger Buckhouse, wanted to keep the administration and running of the fleet in his own hands. Ramsay found that he and his staff were virtually being ignored. He felt that this was a bad state of affairs for the navy – so he resigned his post.

In 1938, he was 'retired' from the navy. Then, at the time of the Munich crisis, with war being a possibility, he was appointed to examine the state of the Dover defences. However, after Munich and with Chamberlin proclaiming that there would be – "Peace with Honour," Ramsay, once again found that his services were – "no longer required." In 1939, with the declaration of war, he was, quickly and 'quietly' appointed Flag Officer in charge, Dover – his retirement was over again!

Once more, Dover found itself a vitally important place on the map, with its harbour, its closeness to France and commanding views of the channel. Should France fall – it was only a 'stepping stone' for the enemy to cross the channel at this point. But since Roman Times though the channel had been too formidable an obstacle for our enemies to have successfully invaded our shores. The naval headquarters at Dover were installed in the corridors and rooms hewn in the chalk of the east cliff, below Dover Castle – they were used in Napoleonic times. In the first World War, one of the rooms had housed an auxiliary electrical plant – a dynamo. Many people believe that Operation Dynamo got its name from this, others believe that 'Dynamo' was next on the list of code names selected for certain operations as they were planned. Whatever the true reason, getting its name from the Dynamo room is the one I know I'm not alone in preferring to believe to be the truth. The atmosphere in the corridors and rooms in the depths of these chalk cliffs, was, to say the least, claustrophobic for Ramsay and his staff – which included quite a few Wrens. (Women's Royal Navy Service).

When Churchill had taken over as prime minister, the general opinion was that he was the right man for the job; but what hardly anyone knew at that critical time in 1940, was anything very much about Ramsay. He seemed a quiet, almost 'stand-offish' man to those that didn't know him, but in fact, he was a smart, efficient, rather small man – also, he was a first class organiser and highly methodical planner who weighed up all the pro's and con's of every situation very carefully. Once again 'fate' seemed to have played a part in putting the right man in the right place at the right time, and exactly the right man to organise the escape of an army from what would soon become – 'the hostile shores just across the water.'

Back on the 20th May, Ramsay had called for a special meeting at Dover, to decide what procedure would be taken in the event of the situation worsening – making it necessary for a wholesale evacuation from France. The main planning for Operation Dynamo then took place – just six days before being brought into effect.

At three o'clock in the afternoon of the 26th of May, Ramsay, in the light of information received from the French coast, had taken matters into his own hands and started to send ships to Dunkirk; by before midnight that night the first troops from the port of Dunkirk were disembarking at Dover – but there were big problems to be faced. Not only were there magnetic minefields to contemplate, but also, at Dunkirk, the harbour was under constant bombardment and ships were being sunk. Ramsay knew that before long, if the port became blocked by wrecks and the quayside severely damaged, the rescue of the B.E.F. would have to continue from the beaches; something that no-one had really contemplated before this, or if they had, dismissed it as – "an impossible task."

Three escape routes were planned, so as to avoid the minefields, and also get some protection from the hard pressed Royal Air Force. These routes were quite simply called – X, Y and Z. Route X meant navigating around some minefields and was 57 miles long. It was not certain whether route Y was mined – this was 87 miles long. Route Z was only 39 miles long, but open to the heaviest air and sea attacks, and consequently it was thought that this could only be used under the cover of dark. Of these routes, Y was thought to be the safest route, even if it did take longer. (See page 50).

The ships available to Ramsay at this time, apart from the destroyers, were mainly made up of merchant ships, cross channel steam packets, (some of which had been converted for mine sweeping duties at the beginning of the war) – coasters, barges and tugs.

The admiralty had informed Ramsay in a signal – 'It was imperative for Dynamo to be implemented with the greatest vigour, with a view to lifting up to 45,000 of the British Expeditionary Force within two days, at the end of which it was probable that evacuation would be terminated by enemy action!'

The scenes in Dunkirk on that tense and frightening Sunday evening were chaotic. Oil tanks were blazing, and the moles (breakwaters) were silhouetted by the light from the flames of burning houses and warehouses. The Luftwaffe were relentless in their bombing raids, and the noise of the bombings and gunfire could be heard in Dover. Ramsay could only guess at that time the immense damage being done to the harbour there, and his mind turned to all the alternative avenues of escape.

The beaches at Dunkirk stretched for miles – indeed, here was the largest stretch of uninterrupted sandy coastline in the whole of Europe, so there was plenty of room for the B.E.F. and if one could get close in shore – a large area for picking up the troops. One of the main

39

difficulties though, would be in ferrying the troops from the shallow waters out to where the larger ships would be waiting to load up as quickly as possible and make their way back to Dover or Ramsgate or elsewhere on the English coastline. It was now that the 'Little Ships' would be needed, and the plan to get them to Ramsgate and Dover ready for their journeys across the channel, was now implemented as well.

The admiralty had already put out a call for any of its officers or ratings, who were used to small craft, to come forward. They would be needed to take charge of many of the boats that the admiralty was now trying to muster up, and take them across the channel.

Back at home, we had recently had a visit from an uncle of mine – my Aunt Daphne's husband, Lt. Nat Vaughn Oliver R.N.V.R. He was not only keen on small craft, but it was his ambition to eventually live on his own boat in some quiet back-water of Sussex. Earlier in the month he had told father, whilst on a short leave, that inquiries were being made for those in the service with small craft experience – but couldn't guess why. Later on, father, in putting two and two together, said to us over the breakfast table one day – "Nat will be involved in this in some way!" He was – but more about him later.

With authority from the admiralty, the call had gone out for suitable small craft to be collected from wherever they could be found and taken to such strategic places as, Sheerness, Ramsgate and Dover. Eventually a large amount of boats were collected from coastal areas – mainly in the south, south-east and east of the country, and also from the rivers and estuaries in those areas. A large amount came from the River Thames – there were quite a variety. Some were luxury craft, some 'lovingly' trying to imitate these, some very ordinary, some 'a bit down at the 'keel' – as one amateur sailor 'jokingly' told me; but all usable – or would be so after a little attention. Many of these were to be found in the non-tidal stretches of the river, from above the locks at Teddington stretching to within sight of the 'Dreaming Spires' of Oxford.

The man asked by a government representative, to choose and organise the collection of these boats was Douglas Tough of 'Tough's Boatyard' at Teddington. Here is how Douglas Tough and his yard became involved in 'Operation Dynamo.'

On May 14th 1940 the B.B.C. made the following announcement:

'The Admiralty have made an order requesting all owners of self propelled pleasure craft, between 30ft. and 100ft. in length to send all particulars to the admiralty within 14 days from today, if they have not already been offered or requisitioned.'

Because of this, the idea of using private yachts or similar boats, kept for the pursuit of pleasure, as naval auxiliaries, was already reasonably well established. With the coming of Dunkirk, there came an absolute order to pick up all the usable boats. The navy once more reverted to press ganging – the difference being that this time it was for the boats, not the men!

Early in the morning of Monday 27th May 1940, Mr. H.C. Riggs, of The Small Craft Section of the Ministry of Shipping, phoned Douglas Tough at Teddington, and asked if he would be willing to act as agent in collecting small craft along the Thames. The need for these little boats was desperate because the coast at Dunkirk, in a line through the beaches at such places as Bray Dunes and La Panne to Nieuport, might be admirable places for spending summer holidays, lazing about on its gently shelving long sandy stretches, but couldn't be approached by the sort of ships required to embark large numbers of troops for the home ports.

Fortunately, the little boats were there – in muddy creeks and estuaries, some in deserted moorings, their owners possibly in uniform or, perhaps just sadly more or less forgotten about and now neglected; some were covered with tarpaulins and some, with their paintwork dirty and brasses tarnished, lay forlornly with water gurgling in their bilge's, almost crying out as if to say – "Here I am, please pay attention to me!" That attention was about to come.

Douglas Tough's responsibility was the Thames Valley, excluding the estuary, and the arrangement was that he, with his chief waterman, Mr. R.H.C. Lenthall and a naval officer, were to go up the river and if they saw a boat, take a close look at it, and if they deemed it would be suitable for the task ahead, they would put a 'crew' on board and take it away. When the owners could be contacted – they were. Some grumbled, but in the main the owners were quick to co-operate – some offering to crew the boats themselves. In the cases where the owners couldn't be contacted, the boats were taken in any case. One boat, after an angry owner had seen it being taken away, was pursued by the police all the way to Teddington Lock, where it was quickly made clear to them that this was with government authority.

More than one hundred of these craft were assembled at The Ferry Road Yard, where Toughs' employees worked hard to prepare them for the sea crossing.

Douglas Tough compiled a list of all the boat owners or others, such as watermen or people just interested in 'mucking about in boats,' who he thought capable and responsible enough to take the boats down river to Sheerness, but with so many boats it required a run of these crews working on rotation to get them all to this destination.

When they arrived at Sheerness the boats were refuelled, and in theory they should have been handed over to navy personnel; however, there weren't enough navy men available, and a lot of civilians took boats across to Dunkirk, though very few took their own boats.

Before telling the stories of some of the boats that came down river from Tough's boatyard, and boats that came from other places, including lifeboats, paddle steamers, barges and tugs, it is necessary to go back to the harbour and beaches of Dunkirk. The harbour, was now becoming increasingly difficult to use, and the soldiers were being directed to the beaches instead. Men were now arriving from all over the place; many of them having earlier on heeded the order – "Every man for himself." They were from a variety of Regiments, and many of them, on trying to find the way to Dunkirk and asking someone – "which way?" – had received the now familiar instructions – "you see where that smoke's coming from? – well, make for that!" These instructions were mainly for men who were ten miles or less from the port, but none the less the smoke could be seen from a long distance away.

Many of the troops were still ignorant of what was going on, or perhaps I should say, most – if not all of them. Some were completely lost and found themselves following others who appeared to have some idea of what direction to take; some of these in small groups – some on their own. The one thing they all had in common, was that they were all heading for the coast and eventually Dunkirk – even if they didn't know it at the time!

One group of four – two from one Regiment and two from another, had got fed up with the indefinite attitude of either their officers or N.C.O's, and without being told – "every man for himself" – had branched off on their own accord; all travelling cross country. They had come together under one roof when less than twenty miles from Dunkirk. They spent an 'extremely comfortable' night in a deserted house, and were lucky enough to have found plenty to eat, and " – enough wine to keep us plastered all the time we were there – I still can't remember how we got to Dunkirk," one of them told me, and went on to say, " – but I can remember spending five hellish days on those beaches just trying to avoid the Stukas. Eventually, two of us, I don't know what happened to the other two, got onto a small boat which took us to a destroyer, which I think was called *H.M.S. Anthony*. Sometime later we arrived in Dover.

Back in France, savaged and confused fighting was going on – in the east, in a line from Comines to Ypres and Nieuport, and in the west from Merville to Cassel and then Gravelines.

By this time there was little or no co-ordination between the British divisions. Of the Germans – from the east, General Bock's Infantry Division pressed relentlessly onwards, and in the west, Rommel's Panzer's, in pincer movements, also relentlessly advanced. The German 'halt' had finished on the 26th May, and by the 28th they were advancing – effectively cutting off six divisions of the French army.

Of the British troops, still trying desperately to fight rearguard actions, by the 29th, Major General Montgomery's 3rd division had withdrawn from the line at Poperinghe – not far from Ypres. Elsewhere, all along the ever constricting front and on the congested roads, the fragmented brigades fought their way in rearguard actions back into the defence perimeter and took up their positions to defend behind the high banks of the canals.

Three days before this, at Dover, Ramsay, realising the confusion there would be on the beaches had appointed Captain W.G. Tennant to – "Go straight to Dover and get the B.E.F. back!" In effect, – a 'Beachmaster.'

43

On the 27th May, Tennant set out from Dover with a party of 12 officers and 150 men in the destroyer *Wolfhound*. The Germans were already shelling the direct route between Dover and Dunkirk, so it was necessary to make a long detour in order to reach Dunkirk – increasing the normal journey of thirty nine miles to one of eighty seven.

Captain Tennant said later, "The sight of Dunkirk and nearby districts gave one a hollow feeling in the pit of the stomach. The Boche had been going for it really hard, and there was not a pane of glass left anywhere – most of it was still lying in the streets. There were also 'unremoved' dead laying about from the last air raid. As regards the bearing and behaviour of the troops, both British and French, prior to and during the embarkation, it must be recorded that the earlier parties were embarked off the beaches in a condition of complete disorganisation. There appeared to be no military officers in charge of the troops, and this impression was undoubtedly enhanced by the difficulty in distinguishing between the uniforms of such officers as were present and those of other ranks. It was soon realised that it was vitally necessary to dispatch naval officers in their unmistakable uniforms, with armed naval beach parties, to take charge of the soldiers on shore immediately prior to embarkation."

It was now becoming very evident how much this sort of organisation was needed; for as far as the eye could see the throng of soldiers on the beaches seemed to increase and multiply as the hours ticked by. At this time, at La Panne, things weren't quite so hectic – as yet, but soon would be; accordingly Tennant had sent an advance party to the beaches there. One member of this particular party, Yeoman/Signaller Victor Chanter has told me his story.

"On May 21st 1940 I left the flagship H.M.S. *Galatea* to return to Chatham Depot Ship, H.M.S. Pembroke, and commenced a course to be made up to trained operator. Whilst in the middle of the exam, a messenger entered to ask me to be kitted out for a special project. After partial kitting procedure, I was allowed back into the examination class to continue the test paper. Within two minutes I was called out again to complete preparations for Dunkirk.

I was issued with webbing, belt, holster and pistol, but there was no one to authorise an issue of ammunition for me. With no time to lose I was 'doubled away' to join a group for transportation to Dover. At Dover, along with others, I boarded *H.M.S. Wolfhound* to cross the channel.

On the approach to Dunkirk we turned east along the coast; and along with several seamen, I was taken inshore by launch. At a point now too shallow for the launch, we scrambled over the side with our gear, I, with Aldis lamp (to be used with any battery I could commandeer from a French vehicle), semaphore flags and a pistol with no ammo, and waded ashore at La Panne. A ball of smoke hung over Dunkirk, and we were to discover that La Panne was to be evacuation headquarters.

Our home for the next few days was to be the beach. There we billeted ourselves on, and were adopted by a Bofers gun crew, until they had to destroy their gun and be evacuated by us.

We commenced organising orderly queues, lines of soldiers for embarkation into small rowing boats and floats; lines which often dispersed quickly into the dunes behind the beach with the arrival of bombs and bursts of machine-gun fire from German aircraft strafing the sands.

Commandeering floatable personnel-carrying material was at a premium owing to the lack of boats and rafts – once a troop-laden craft had reached the comparative safety of an awaiting rescue ship offshore, we could hardly expect volunteers to row back to shore with it. Some abandoned boats did drift back to be rescued by us for further use.

All troops for evacuation were ordered by us to abandon every bit of surplus kit to allow for space; rifles not used for rowing purposes were to be destroyed. That didn't go down well with some of the squaddies.

In the early days it proved difficult to get some of the soldiers to wade out before attempting to get into the boats; some of the boats became overloaded, sticking in the sand. At this point it was almost impossible to persuade anyone to jump out to lighten the load; though we tried to assure them that we would allow them back in once we could reach deeper water.

On one occasion three of us (R.N.) had just managed to re-float a full-to-the-gunwale cutter. "O.k. Row like hell! Get going!" We

45

screamed at them. We turned and made for shore, wading to our armpits in the water. At that moment I heard and felt an almighty bang, and as I fell forward into the sea, I knew I'd been hit on the back of the head. I surfaced and the situation became clear, and later, a bit of a laugh.

The soldiers in the boat had responded well to our order to 'get going!' but on one side only. Consequently the cutter swung round ninety degrees, got caught up in a swell and came down on you-know-who. I guess the lads in the boat got home somehow!

It's obvious that we R.N. lads were consistently getting wet through but we were never short of a change of uniform. All over the beach was the pick of the army – discarded uniforms, photos, everything! Perhaps some lucky ones found time to grab the few most treasured possessions that they could cram into their battledress pockets, but for most it was the time for survival and leaving old memories behind. So, sadly at times, whilst looking for dry clothing to put on; searching through the discarded packs strewn along the sands, I would come upon family photographs; wives and children looking out at me, a complete stranger! Indications of haste and urgency required that a soldier couldn't stop to salvage from his own belongings the very few personal articles that were his alone – and not issued to him.

One hoped that the owners of these keepsakes would soon be united with the ones in the photographs. Not all of them would make it to England, and those that did – how long would it be before they were away again to some other theatre of war?

After the first day or so at La Panne we began to receive motorised units. Then a new stratagem was devised. At low tide the highest vehicles were driven out to a given point, and by driving and parking other trucks alongside, a pier was formed from which the troops were able to clamber into the boats that could now come alongside.

This procedure was a welcome break to us. First we had the organisation of the structure, between bouts of shelling, low level bombing and machine gunning from enemy aircraft, and then we had the easier filling of the boats; no more brute force required pushing the boats out and getting wet through.

I know that none of the R.N. personnel knew just how much energy was spent during those sleepless hours and days – the army, by the time it had reached the beach, had already expended so much energy – we of the R.N. landing party had arrived fresh upon the beach. Frequent 24 hours of servicing boats did nothing to diminish the enthusiasm for the job; but enthusiasm doesn't compensate completely for spent energy. We were therefore thankful for the labour saving piers we helped to build.

So good was the organisation that the troops were able to embark sometimes under orders of a senior army officer, with fewer directives from us. We could now spend more time with our own group and discuss the future: H.Q. Staff at La Panne, plus General Gort, would at some time soon have to be evacuated. We had also to consider making provision for our own escape procedure.

It was at one of these get-togethers – a foray into the Bofors gun crew's rations – that a direct hit on one of our piers was made by a German bomber. Reading about such an occurrence is one thing, but experiencing such frustration is something else. The lads waiting there on the pier, ready to be taken off next for their journey back home, had been so close! We no longer joked 'Anyone for the Skylark?' The gap in our pier was never filled in!

We also had more time to watch where the enemy shells landed as they screamed overhead. (If you hear them they've missed you!) Mostly they went over the beach towards the rescue ships lying off. A lot of harsh words were said around us at this time; but no one said it was going to be easy. We did see a couple of dog fights, but nothing to stop the strafing of the beaches, the bombing and machine gunning, and nothing to stop the enemy from receiving information from the German recce aircraft about our troop and shipping movements."

There is more about Vic later in the book.

In the meantime, out to sea, the destroyers were giving covering fire for the steamers and other commercial ships which were embarking troops from the beaches – they were giving a good account of themselves in shelling the German shore batteries. Soon, these destroyers would be used for bringing troops back as well.

47

At Dover, Ramsay found himself under constant pressure from the admiralty, who felt that the extra destroyers that Dover wanted were better used for defending the merchant ships in the Atlantic. They reasoned that going near to Dunkirk was 'suicidal' for the destroyers. Some had already been sunk, resulting in some of the newest ones being withdrawn from the action at Dunkirk. However, after two valuable days without these ships, and Ramsay's never relenting demands that – "I must have more destroyers!" – He eventually, necessarily, got them back.

Before the little ships came to take their part in the evacuation, paddle steamers also came to help – These were familiar sights in peacetime in such resorts as Brighton, Margate, Ramsgate, Southend and other seaside towns. Some of them had already been doing fine work after being requisitioned by the navy and converted for such duties as minesweeping – they were now to play an integral part in Operation Dynamo. Also, there were the cross channel boats of Southern Railways, with such ships as the *Normania, Maid of Kent, Isle of Thanet, Canterbury, Maid of Orleans, Whitstable*, and many more.

A number of these had been chartered from the beginning of the war by The Admiralty and used as military transports, and in particular, as hospital ships. Some of the ships had already been lost before Operation Dynamo began; one of them – the *Maid of Kent* – whilst loaded with wounded, was hit by bombs and sunk in the harbour at Dieppe. At this time also, reports were coming in of ships being sunk in mid-channel and the survivors being picked up by other ships ferrying troops.

By the night of 28th/29th May, with even more ships now coming to take men off from the Mole and other places, Captain Tennant estimated that they were loading up to 200 troops an hour. The Luftwaffe however, were increasing their activities as well and the whole operation was becoming ever more tricky, as well as more dangerous.

On the 28th May, the good news was that the Admiralty had released to Ramsay all destroyers that were already in home waters. However, this was a sad day for some of the ships, including the popular Paddle Steamers, *Gracie Fields* and *Brighton Belle*. The stories of these 'little ships' and another paddle steamer that came to pick up the survivors from the *Brighton Belle*, I feel should be told in some detail – they are stories that will be forever etched in accounts of the rescues from Dunkirk.

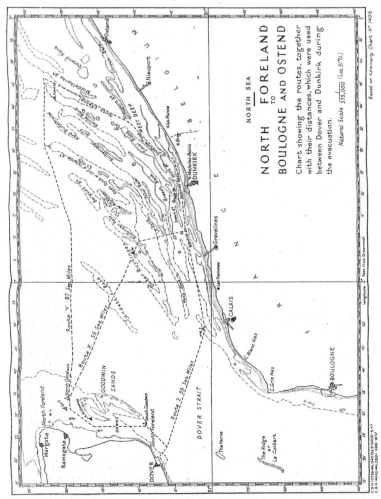

Sea routes for Operation Dynamo

50

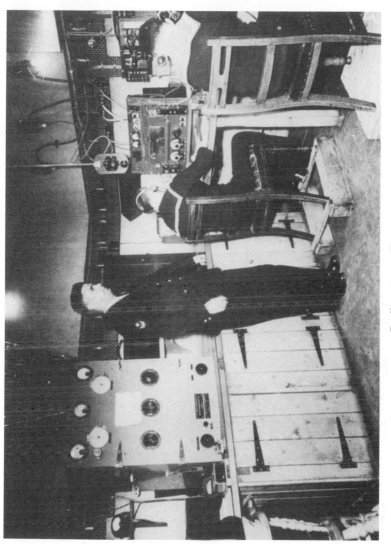

Radio room at Dover

51

Troops leaving the jetty at Dunkirk Harbour

'Destroyer at the mole – quite early in the evacuation'
(Imperial War Museum – H.U. 1153)

Dunkirk – A sinister scene
(Imperial War Museum – H.U. 2286)

Craft of all kinds – crammed full

A confusion of ships and men 'Ready to unload'

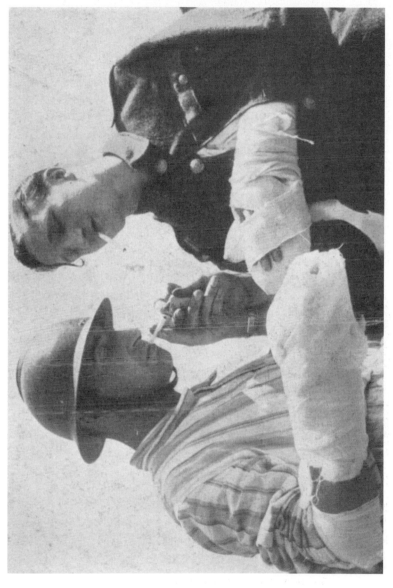

French soldier – British 'Tommy'

Helping hand for a 'veteran'

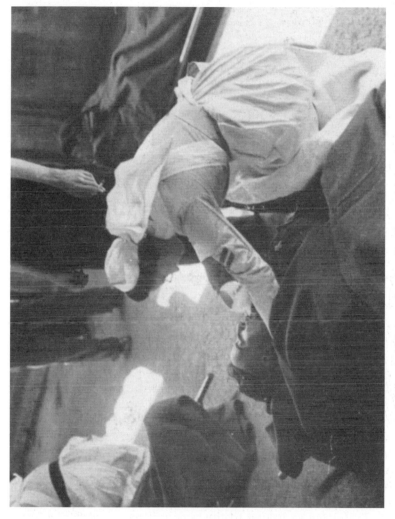

Nurse at hand – A welcome drink

Chapter Four

Steamers and Beachboats

In an interesting booklet of words and pictures published in aid of The Red Cross in 1940, the author, J.B. Priestley, allowed them to print an introductory passage taken from a broadcast he had made on the B.B.C. about the Dunkirk rescue operations. Here are some of the words that they chose from his broadcast:

"– Here at Dunkirk is another English epic. And to my mind what was most characteristically English about it – so typical of us, so absurd and yet so grand and gallant when you hardly know whether to laugh or cry when you read about them – was the part played in the difficult and dangerous embarkation, not by the warships, magnificent though they were, but by the little pleasure steamers. We have known them and laughed at them, these fussy little steamers, all our lives. We have called them 'the shilling sicks.' We have watched them load and unload their crowds of holiday passengers – the gents full of high spirits and bottled beer, the ladies eating pork pies, the children sticky with peppermint rock. Sometimes they only went as far as the next seaside resort. But the boldest of them might manage a channel crossing to let everybody have a glimpse of Boulogne. They were usually paddle-steamers, making a great deal more fuss with all their churning than they made speed; and they weren't proud, for they let you see their works going round. They liked to call themselves 'Queens and Belles;' and even if they were new, there was always something old fashioned, a Dickens touch, a mid Victorian air, about them. They seem to belong to the same ridiculous holiday world as peirrots and piers, sand castles, ham-and-egg teas, palmists, automatic machines and crowded sweating promenades.

But they were called out of that world – and, let it be noted, they were called out in good time and in good order, Yes, these *Brighton Belles* and *Brighton Queens* left that innocent foolish world of theirs to sail into the inferno, to defy bombs, shells, magnetic mines, torpedoes, machine-gun fire – to rescue our soldiers. Some of them, alas! Will never return. Amongst those paddle-steamers that will never return was one that I knew well, for it was the pride of the ferry service to the Isle of Wight – none other than the good ship *Gracie Fields.–*"

I will put the remainder of Mr. Priestley's talk in the epilogue. Jim Cockfield, who at the time of Dunkirk was in the 50th Northumbrian Division, H.Q. – R.A.O.C. was on board the *Gracie Fields* when she was bombed – briefly, here is what happened:

Jim had gone to France with his regiment in December 1939. They had got as far as Brussels on their journey into Belgium in 1940 when it was all change – retreat instead of advance. They spent some time – most of it in transport, but the last miles on foot – making their way to the beach at La Panne. After spending some time there looking for some form of transport to take them across the water back to England, he, with some others, got on a rowing boat which then headed for a large ship they could see lying offshore. The rowing boat was damaged somehow – "something to do with the seams." Jim told me. So they changed course and headed for a paddle steamer, which at that moment seemed closer to them. This turned out to be the *Gracie Fields* – they were quickly taken on board.

The *Gracie Fields* had been launched in 1936 by the famous entertainer she had been named after. Gracie had sung 'Sing As We Go,' at the ceremony – a song that became synonymous with her name. The launching had been at Woolston on the river Itchen – she had been designed to be suitable for the run from Southampton to Cowes, on the Isle of Wight.

In 1936, her first season, she made a special trip to Brighton – Gracie had a special interest in an orphanage at Peacehaven, just to the east of Brighton, and she arrived there one day to take the children on a pre-arranged outing on the paddle steamer.

My mother had a good friend who was a voluntary helper at this children's home, and she had asked mother whether she could spare the day helping them with the children on this cruise – she accepted gladly – "A day to remember." She told father afterwards.

The steamer's popular peacetime master – Captain N.R. Larkin, had stayed on with her, with the rank of Lieutenant when she had been taken over by the Royal Navy and converted as a minesweeper at the beginning of the war – she became part of the 10th Flotilla at Dover.

Jim told me that shortly after they got on board, they went to dry their clothing in the engine room. Sometime later the ship was bombed and the engine room hit; fortunately Jim was unscathed, but unfortunately several men were killed. Jim says, "There was steam everywhere and the rudder had jammed, so we started going round and round in circles." Earlier on the *Gracie Fields* had loaded up with 750 troops from the beaches at La Panne – the day before this, the 27th May, she had picked up 281 men and taken them to Dover. They were still circling when two 'skoots' came to take some of the men off. Jim got on one of these – the *Jutland*. The sloop *Pangbourne* took off the remainder of the men and then took the stricken *Gracie Fields* in tow. Unfortunately this necessitated that their progress was very slow, and during the night, the paddle steamer filled with water, and with the last of her crew, including Lt. Larkin, taken safely off – she sank. Later in the operation, the *Jutland* was also sunk.

My grandfather, Albert Redhead, having sold his farm near Peterborough, bought number thirteen Sussex Square in Brighton in the early 1920's. Before becoming a farmer, grandfather had served in The Royal Navy, and had always been a keen amateur sailor – a good one, he had once sailed single handed around the British Isles. He never lost his love of the sea. In his later life, he liked going on trips on the 'old steam packets' that were in operation around the south east of England, and knew quite a few of the crew members on these holiday craft. His favourite was *The Brighton Belle* – he and my grandmother often used to take their four, at that time nearly grown up children, on trips on what grandmother described as – "that lovely, cosy little ship."

My father had married my mother in 1927, and they lived in the top flat at number thirteen – the flat eventually to be taken over by

Bruce Belfrage and his family early in 1940. In the days before I was born, my parents often went for trips on *The Brighton Belle* – a boat that they came to think of – "As our own!" Their memories of trips aboard her were all very happy ones, and father had organised small parties to go from The Army Officers Hospital on the seafront, for day trips. On one occasion, on a men only outing, coming home somewhat the worse for wear, not from seasickness but from too much alcohol taken with his friends during their special day. I never set foot on this old paddle steamer myself, but I like to think that perhaps father had prematurely 'wet the baby's head' aboard her.

During *The Brighton Belle's* life, there were just two occasions when my parents were saddened by news about her. The first was in 1933 – the year I was born – when she was withdrawn from service at Brighton and the Sussex coast and put to work by her owners, P. & A. Campbell, on the Bristol Channel.

The second occasion was during the evacuation from Dunkirk, when the news came through that she had been sunk. Here is the story of *The Brighton Belle* on that fateful day – 28th May 1940, and also the story of the ship that came to help – *The Medway Queen*.

The steamer, *Lady Evelyn*, was built in 1900. In 1923 she had been renamed – *Brighton Belle*, after being taken over by P. & A. Campbell. She had then spent the next ten years on the Sussex coast, until being transferred to work on The Bristol Channel.

When war broke out in 1939, all pleasure trips stopped and *The Brighton Belle* – like quite a few other steamers – found herself taken over by the navy and fitted out as a minesweeper. She soon joined The Tenth Flotilla based at Dover. She was kept very busy during the winter of 1939/1940 on duty in the channel. That time might have been the phoney war to many 'landlubbers' – but to the navy, especially in the channel and in the Atlantic – this was a time of great vigilance.

On the evening of the 27th May 1940, with the evacuation of the troops from Dunkirk about to come into full swing, and after the go-ahead for 'Operation Dynamo' the day before, The *Brighton Belle* made for Dunkirk and filled up with nearly 800 troops. Early on the 28th she left the harbour and – carefully avoiding the wrecks of recently bombed ships – made her way out into the channel for the

63

home shores. Whilst approaching the north Goodwins she came to the attention of some enemy aircraft, and in taking avoiding action, *The Brighton Belle* hit a submerged wreck – it was sadly the end of her! Before she sank though, other ships came to her rescue, but it was *The Medway Queen* who came alongside her as she settled by the stern.

The brave crew of *The Medway Queen*, now under fire themselves from enemy aircraft, managed to get the troops and crew off quickly and make for Dover. In returning the fire whilst all this was going on, they succeeded in bringing down one of the enemy aircraft.

The Medway Queen started life at Ailsa's Yard in Troon, Scotland. She was one of the finest and most luxurious paddle steamers built to provide excursions in the Thames and Medway estuaries. She was much loved by the thousands who sailed in her, until in 1939, she was called up to serve with the navy as part of the 10th Minesweeping Flotilla. She was originally designed to carry almost a thousand passengers, and could make a speed of 15 knots.

H.M.S. *Medway Queen's* naval service started in the bitter winter of 1939/40, yet her new crew came to love her and were soon welded into an efficient fighting force as part of the Dover Patrol.

On May 28th 1940, she was anchored off the south coast, spotting where enemy aircraft were 'laying' mines, when she was ordered to proceed to the beaches of Dunkirk. It was shortly after this when *The Medway Queen* added the troops from *The Brighton Belle* to her already substantial load. The day after this, *The Medway Queen* was once again steaming for Dunkirk from Dover, and under her captain, Lieutenant A.T. Cook R.N.R. with Sub/Lt. J.D. Graves R.N.R. as her second in command, they entered the harbour of Dunkirk amid heavy fire. On shore, the oil tanks were ablaze by then and there was wreckage everywhere. Scaling ladders were used to enable troops to come down to the ship from the Mole, high above them, and she was soon full again. Lieutenant Jolly, her navigator throughout the operation, quickly got her under way. They slipped over the mine fields to save time, relying on their shallow draft to avoid destruction. As night fell, her crew devised ingenious ways to subdue the phosphorescence in the water with oil, to escape enemy detection. This time they returned to Ramsgate. Once more, they refuelled and took on all the stores that they could carry. Now they went back alternately to the harbour and the beaches of Dunkirk. On the beaches, they had the use of their motorised dinghy to bring the troops out. Once aboard, the men were taken care of by *The Medway Queen's* extraordinary cook, Thomas Russell, who, with his assistant, took pride in caring for the soldiers with food and drinks – but more about him soon.

I think I can hardly do justice to *The Medway Queen* and those that sailed in her without including the following accounts of some of her crew. The first by Bruce Sutton:

'One afternoon in May 1940 *The Medway Queen* left Dover for the continent where our forces were in trouble. A long time before we got there we saw the flames, and soon we smelled the fuel oil. No person who was there will forget it. We went six more times, mostly to La Panne beach, but sometimes in Dunkirk harbour going around the many wrecks.

We had a motor boat which towed another one to and fro from the beach. The army lined up on the shore – I did not see anyone panic or jump the queue. When the ship returned to Ramsgate, ladies were waiting with tea and sandwiches and our passengers were whisked away. We refuelled, stored, tidied up and it was time to go again. On one trip we came back in company with *The Brighton Belle*; she hit a wreck – we went alongside and they all came aboard before she sank. Fortunately it was a calm day as we were very overloaded, but we got home okay. At one time it was reported by the BBC that we had sunk, but they later said that it was another ship. The way over was marked by small boats that had been abandoned.'

The second account by a crew member is written by Sub/Lt. Graves – he writes:

"On the way in that second night the sea was unusually phosphorescent. Our paddles left broad twin wakes, and on two occasions German aircraft followed these wakes 'till their end and dropped bombs uncomfortably close. We were nothing if not resourceful aboard *The Medway Queen* and devised oil bags which were lowered over the bow on 'either side' just as they are used at sea to break the force of heavy waves. This was most successful, our brilliant wakes disappeared and *Medway Queen* went her way in decent obscurity again, but, at the most critical point of the trip,

65

when we were creeping along the French coast past Gravelines, the funnel began to stream sparks, caused by deposited soot catching fire. We were cross with the chief engineer – but there was nothing he could do about it. However, those sparks made the ship a very obvious target and they had to be supressed. There then followed an hilarious half hour, set against the tragic background of burning Dunkirk. A bucket chain was formed from the main deck and up the ladders to the part of the flying bridge which approached the funnel. Our tallest sailor took the buckets of water and tried to tip their contents down the funnel, either to put out the fire or at least to damp it down. This was reasonably successful, but not much appreciated by the engine room staff. At one stage a voice from the gloomy depths of the funnel proclaimed " I do not intend to be ******* well drowned on the job!"

The Harbour that night presented the appearance, to become all too familiar, of the wreck of one of the most modern ports in Europe. Docks and Quay walls were rubble, and torn and broken ships lay everywhere. One single pier remained – the outer Mole on the north side of the Harbour. Never designed for handling goods or allowing the passage of men, it was all that was left, and the navy decided to use it. It can be said of that concrete strip on its concrete piles that it helped save Britain and the free world. Along its length walked, stumbled or were carried very nearly a quarter of a million men during the nine days of the evacuation. Ships were sunk alongside it, putting parts out of use. Lengths of it were torn away by shell or bomb. The gaps were repaired by mess tables from ships, by ladders, wood planking and other material taken from the debris around the Harbour, and all the time, silhouetted by the flames at night and looking drawn and tired by day, that weary file of men stumbled along its length.

Many types of ships made fast to that mole. Destroyers with their advantages of speed and manoeuverability, played a significant part, but there were also the personnel carriers, as the pre-war cross channel ships were described, and the hospital ships, the trawlers, the drifters, the Dutch Skoots – every variety of small ship, civilian and naval, and of course the Paddle Minesweepers. All in their turn came, filled up and went, and let it be said there was never any distinction between nationalities or services. All who came were taken. Any man who presented himself abreast the ship was embarked. Only civilian families were excluded. The rule was firmly enforced. These were hard times and had it become known that transport to Britain was available, crowds of refugees might have turned up to their own great danger and the exclusion of men needed to defend our Island. Priority had to be given to fighting soldiers.

In the meantime, whilst all this was going on above decks – below decks, cook, Thomas Russell, was working like a man possessed. Here is an excerpt from his own account:

"I swayed on sore feet, my head ached abominably and my body was wracked with fatigue, as up until then I had had no sleep for 72 hours. It was 4 a.m. – the end of a bandage was dipping in the mess-tin which was held out to me, but I was unable to stop my robot-like 'dip and pour' rhythm in time to avoid emptying a ladle of stew over it. Curiosity made me look up and some drops of perspiration fell from the end of my nose into the stew. The soldier I saw was wounded in the head, his young face pinched and white under the blood-soaked field dressing. Blood and sweat. They were certainly fitting symbols of the harrowing event we were experiencing and the manner of its achievement, I thought.

Our eyes met as, reaching out, he removed the bandage, then heartily sucked the gravy from the end of it before tucking it back in place. It was a savage gesture and I wondered when he had eaten last. He grinned at me as if it hurt his lips to stretch them.

"Thanks, pal. Tastes smashing."

I returned his smile wearily and hoped it conveyed to him – 'not to mention it, it was my pleasure.' However, he was only one of the seemingly endless queue of men who were clamouring for food and there was soon another mess-tin awaiting to be filled. And another – and another – would the nightmare never end?"

On one of the trips *The Medway Queen* made, she picked up one man who was literally swimming for his life. John Howarth was with the 2nd Division, Ammunition Company of the R.A.S.C. They were advancing into Belgium when all of a sudden they came upon troops – "going the other way!" It wasn't long after this, in all the confusion, that the order was – 'every man for himself!' He and

67

some of the other men got various lifts on the retreat, until they got to Poperinghe, where lifts became difficult to get. They started walking and eventually after they'd been on the go for about twenty miles, they ended up on the beach at Bray Dunes.

"We spent two hellish days here – we were continuously dived bombed." John said. Eventually we were told to make for some little boats we could see coming in, and myself, a Grenadier sergeant and four French soldiers got on one of these. It was manned by a father and son, I believe – in any case they were civillians. A bit later, when we were well out into The Channel, we were attacked by enemy aircraft, and sunk. The Frenchmen and the father and son were sadly killed. This left just me and the sergeant in the water. We swam about for what seemed to be hours – I think I'd more or less given up hope by then – when all of a sudden our rescuers came on the scene in the shape of the *The Medway Queen*. There is a little more about the *Medway Queen* later in the book and in the epilogue.

On Tuesday 28th May, the Thames paddle steamer *Crested Eagle* was attacked by Stukas. The first bombs missed but then a bomb made a direct hit on the ship, just forward of the bridge; two further bombs set the fuel tanks ablaze – the *Crested Eagle* quickly became a blazing inferno. Her captain, Lieutenant – Commander Booth managed to beach her, but many had died.

One of the soldiers who witnessed this from the beach was Arthur Oates of the 145th Brigade, 48th South Midlands Division of the R.A.S.C. Before arriving on the beaches, one of his jobs had been delivering rations to the 145th Field Ambulance Company. During the retreat he remembers driving up to a NAAFI warehouse at Lille – there was no-one there, so they loaded up with all manner of food items, as well as drinks and cigarettes, which they then carried to Bray Dunes and shared out amongst the troops there. Arthur, in his letter to me says, "That afternoon on the beach I saw at least one destroyer bombed and sunk; then the paddle steamer *Crested Eagle* was hit and beached a few hundred yards away from us. At the same time as this we were machine gunned, and had to make quickly for the dunes."

The next morning Arthur and some of his mates found an empty rowing boat, which they successfully rowed out to a destroyer, which later took them to Dover.

Two other soldiers and two other boats come into the story at this time. The men are Norman Lees and Albert Atkinson; they came home on different boats, but the boats shared something in common – they were both called *Bullfinch*.

Many years later, Mike Twyman of The Margate Historical Society, after much research, eventually 'sorted out' the truth that there were two boats with this name – both of which went to Dunkirk!

The boat Norman Lees had boarded at the mole at Dunkirk, was The Royal Fleet Auxiliary Cable laying vessel – *Bullfinch*. She had been launched in March 1940, and as Norman says – "there was still the smell of fresh paint about her." This is Norman's story:

He had grown up in Manchester at a time when everybody seemed to be either a cotton worker or an engineer. The only holidays available to him in those times during the 1920's and 30's, was with a pal's aunt who had moved to Broadstairs – she invited the boys to come and stay with her and this was to be Norman's first experience of the delights of nearby Margate – the second one was to be very different!

On the evening of May 28th 1940, Norman, a private in the Cheshire Regiment, found himself caught up in the shambles that was the retreat to Dunkirk. By 7 p.m. that evening he was 12 miles inland from Dunkirk, assisting an injured pal towards the coast. By one means or another they found themselves in Dunkirk in the late evening. He recalls that a shirt-sleeved naval officer directed them onto the mole where the vessel *Bullfinch* was moored and loading troops. Negotiating the temporary repairs which had been made to the mole following the Luftwaffe's concerted efforts to bomb it out of existence, Norman got his pal down a vertical ladder, with the help of the crew of *Bullfinch*, and straight away negotiated another vertical ladder down into the after hold of the vessel. Norman says that the night was dark but down in the hold, where men stood shoulder to shoulder, packed like sardines – there was an inky blackness. He and his companion were the very last to board and a few minutes later, at around 11 p.m., *Bullfinch* slipped away from the mole and headed seawards. After what seemed to him to be about ten minutes, the vessel was shaken by enormous explosions – "just outside" as he puts it. As the troops realised that they were below the water line, Norman says "there was nothing to do but gulp and

69

wait." A message was passed down from the bridge, the comforting assurance that – "the German's are using our wake as an aiming point!" Eventually the planes gave up, but *Bullfinch* was now dead in the water her engine stopped. Another message came from the bridge, "the steering is damaged but we're trying to correct this." The bombs had damaged the rudder and we wallowed off Dunkirk for what seemed an eternity to the men in the hold. Now and again the engine would start up for a brief spell and then shut down again. All this time the men could hear the sounds of other vessels passing and the fear of being run down in the dark was another worry as *Bullfinch* had left her lifeboats at Dunkirk to help on the beaches. At last, the engine ticked over for ten minutes and then it was full speed ahead, much to the relief of all.

The men did not know their destination. Some were of the opinion that they would be heading for another French port, but most hoped that it would be England and home. Norman recalls that he was standing at the bottom of the ladder, where he had squeezed in on boarding, and was looking up to the deck where some men were watching the daybreak. He could easily hear their voices and one said – "Look, there's a flashing light." He went up the ladder to join them saying – "I'm a signaller, where's that light?" He then had a brief moment of panic as he imagined being overwhelmed by a torrent of flashing signals, but he need not have worried, it was quite easy. The signal read – 'To *Bullfinch* from Ramsgate. No berthing Ramsgate proceed to Margate;' they had made it safely back home.

Soon, *Bullfinch* was moored alongside the jetty at Margate, discharging her cargo of 600 weary but grateful men. Norman says that the Margatonians there to greet them, looked amazed at their condition and the troops were equally surprised to see folk with scrubbed faces and ironed clothes.

So, at 5 a.m. on 29th May 1940, Norman made his second visit to Margate with companions speaking in dialects from all over Britain, and belonging to Regiments from The Northumberland Fusiliers to The Buffs, but only himself and his pal from Cheshire.

The other ship with the same name, was the motor vessel *Bullfinch* owned by The General Steam Navigation Company and built in

Scotland in 1936. She had been sent by order of the Admiralty to La Panne beach, and eventually loaded up 800 troops from Bray Dunes. Once *Bullfinch* had floated off from the dunes and started for home, she suffered several near misses from bombs at the stern. The concussion from the blasts damaged a circuit breaker, causing it to fly open and put the rudder out of action.

Albert Atkinson, a member of The 237/60th Field Regiment Royal Artillery, had been one of those taken on board. He says – "As the troops had come onboard they were asked to empty their .303 ammunition out of their pouches into a six foot galvanised bath, before being sent below for shelter, as the Germans were attacking almost non stop. The only people allowed to remain on deck were Albert and his two magazine loaders, Ken Simpson and Bill Reynolds, both of whom Albert sent below as the planes attacked. The loaders had prepared about fifty magazines for the gun, for which Albert had no proper stand – so he aimed the Bren by resting it on the lifeboat davits as the planes came in to attack. During the time he manned the gun he shot down three Stuka dive bombers; two they saw crash into the sea, the third heading off, trailing smoke whilst losing altitude.

After being damaged, *The Bullfinch* had spent an anxious time immobilised; it drifted towards Dunkirk – she was trapped between two minefields. Eventually, the vessel's engineers managed to fix the damage and she once more made tracks for home.

On arrival at Ramsgate Albert was 'chaired' ashore, along with his Bren-gun, by his mates and the crew of *The Bullfinch*.

With the 'little ships' now coming to take their part in the evacuation, word soon came back that even more boats were desperately needed to take the troops off the beaches to the larger ships lying off shore.

At Deal on the 28th May, the call came for as many suitable boats as possible to proceed forthwith to Ramsgate. On arrival there, the crews of the Deal beach boats, *Golden Spray, Moss Rose, Brittanic, Rose Marie* and *Lady Haig*, were told that they wouldn't be required to take their own boats over, and given railway warrants to get them back to Deal. This didn't go down too well – Dick Brown the skipper of *Lady Haig* was particularly angry, and pointed out to the naval officer in charge at Ramsgate that they all wished to take their own boats over. Unfortunately the request was denied.

The *Lady Haig* – just 27ft long – was actually a hoveller; that is an unlicensed, privately owned lifeboat. Her chief occupation though was fishing.

When war had been declared, because of Deal's position geographically, some of the boats there had been kept extremely active giving assistance to any boats needing it in that very busy stretch of the channel near to them, which includes the treacherous and notorious Goodwin Sands.

Two of the Deal boats did go over with their own crews however – these were *Golden Spray II* and *Gipsy King*. One of the crew on board *Golden Spray* was seventy years of age. Both these boats and the others manned by R.N. personnel, made many trips rescuing troops from the beaches at Dunkirk to the larger ships laying offshore.

There is one very coincidental story concerning the *Lady Haig*. As I have said, Dick Brown was very disappointed at not being allowed to take this boat over to Dunkirk, but under its naval crew, they rescued many troops from the beaches; these included two Grenadier Guardsmen – brothers, Alfred and Jim Redman. They were the nephews of Dick Brown, and cousins of Jim Brown, who in a recent talk with me at the Maritime Museum at Deal, gave me much useful information concerning the Deal boats at the time of Dunkirk. Jim, a captain in The Trinity House Service, retired a few years back; he was one of it's most respected masters.

At 23.00 hours on 27th May, King Leopold of the Belgians accepted truce terms with Germany. This was despite frantic efforts from the French High Command, and from London an invitation from Winston Churchill to be flown here to discuss matters first. Leopold's promises had meant nothing, and in seeking a truce with Germany in such circumstances, it is difficult to describe in full what this meant at the time – although the descriptions, general confusion, horror and being badly let down, readily spring to mind.

The papers had a field day on this, but at least 'the man in the street' was now starting to get in touch with the realities of just how bad things really were.

In The Times on the 29th May, they printed what various prominent people in the government had to say on the matter. Perhaps typical of the remarks made by those who were given the time to have their say, came from Lord Marchwood. He said:

"The leader of the house has asked us to withhold judgment, and he is right in doing so, but I feel that the position is so grave that history will say that the action of the King of The Belgians is that of a base, cowardly traitor at the present time."

Back at home, father's comments on the situation were typical of what was on most peoples lips – disgust and amazement! Mother was now even more worried about the whereabouts of her brother, but at least was unselfish in her appraisal of the situation by saying " – There must be people all over the country feeling like this today, and I feel for them too."

She was right there; The British Expeditionary Force were certainly at the business end of things, but back at home, in practically every street in the UK, there were wives, mothers, sweethearts and other relatives and close friends, who were all now praying for a loved one's safe return, and total attention now focused on how an army was to be rescued from the 'dark lands' across the channel.

Chapter Five

Trains and Boats and Planes

W ith the troops now arriving back at the British ports, the army and other authorities were faced with the task of transporting them to various bases all over the country, and this is where Southern Railways came to take their part.

The Southern Railways main role was that of carrying troops by train when they had landed in England, but they also supplied many ships that played highly important parts in the rescue.

The biggest headache they had to start with on the trains, was not knowing what numbers they were going to be transporting to different places – in other words what trains and how many staff would be required. Also, at that time, they had no idea of where they were supposed to be transporting them to, and to make things even worse, the military, with all the secrecy going on, might change their minds about the direction the train was going – whilst on route! "It reminded me of the station master in that old film 'The Ghost Train' when he said – 'Where do they come from and where do they go?' – " One old railwayman who had helped at the time, told me.

When things had looked at their grimmest across the channel, Mr. Churchill later told a packed House of Commons, he had expected 20,000 to 30,000 to be rescued – not the eventual 335,000.

With great foresight however, Southern Rail supplied an adequate amount of trains, and by dawn on 27th May a 'procession' had begun, with one train quickly following another and moving off to destinations unknown to the hungry, thirsty, exhausted and 'tattered' men on board them – and the whole thing worked like clockwork.

By this time the cross-channel boats of Southern Railways, with names such as – *Normania, Canterbury, Maid of Kent, Whitstable,*

74

Worthing, Isle of Thanet, Paris, Maid of Orleans and more, were already playing important roles in the evacuations. Some of them had been chartered by the Admiralty from the beginning of the war, to be used either as military transports or as hospital ships. Sadly, Some, including *The Paris*, were sunk. This is what happened to two others of these ships – *Canterbury and Maid of Orleans.*

In the early stages of the evacuations, *Canterbury* had proved the potential of the passenger ships by taking off 1,246 men at Dunkirk's Gare Maritime. These were mainly made up of base personnel who were no longer required.

On the 27th May, with the enemy action increasing, *Canterbury* reached Dunkirk at 8.00 p.m., and quickly loaded 457 troops, most of them wounded – including 140 stretcher cases. It took just 58 minutes to load up, during which time the bombing was continuous – indeed, so bad that the captain had orders to turn back any vessel trying to reach Dunkirk that night, and she did turn back the *Maid of Orleans* and two hospital ships; one of these – *Isle of Thanet*, had a collision on her way home which temporarily put her out of action. The return journey was made even more hazardous by the constant dropping of parachute flares by enemy aircraft. On her third journey, on the 29th May, *Canterbury* had left with nearly 2,000 troops on board – they had been loaded during a ferocious air raid and the ship suffered extensive damage, which would have to be repaired before making a fourth and final journey later on.

Some of the story of the *Maid of Orleans* I have in more detail thanks to some correspondence from James Tooley of Orpington, whose father George Tooley was second engineer on board her. He writes:

"My father, George Frederick Tooley, a marine engineer, came south to work for the then Southern Railway in 1929. I was approaching my eighth birthday when war was declared, so my recollections are limited, but I do recall the family gathered around our radio at our home in Folkestone to listen to the famous Chamberlain broadcast. We had already prepared an air raid shelter in a cellar under the house which opened out into the garden, so, after the broadcast we put our gas masks on and went down to the cellar to wait for the bombs to fall – they didn't, and before long everything returned to normal.

At the time of Dunkirk, my father was second engineer of the *Maid of Orleans*, but as the Chief Engineer went sick, he was Acting Chief Engineer throughout the evacuation. They made many trips, bringing back thousands of troops, before colliding with a destroyer and having to retire to dry dock at Southampton. This is George Tooley's own account:

'From the beginning of May 1940, until the Germans invaded Holland, *S.S. Maid of Orleans* lay in the port of Rotterdam. At last, orders arrived quite suddenly, instructing us to proceed to Dover, and we made our departure with relief in having escaped the German trap, though regret at leaving behind our companion. *S.S. St. Denys*, which later had to be scuttled.

Steaming southwards towards the Dunkirk roads, we had several visits from a Junkers 88 which indulged in some fortunately inaccurate bombing.

To the north of Dunkirk and in the roads to port and starboard, were anchored two lines of shipping which stretched as far as the eye could see. It was obvious that their passage to ports further north was now halted. Flanked on either side of this evidence of an abrupt end to the 'phoney' war, we realised that some formidable movement was under way further afield.

On arrival at Dover, we lay at the eastern arm of the breakwater until ordered to sail to Boulogne with gas bottles for the balloon barrage defence. The futility of this operation became apparent when, on reaching the port and swinging inside the breakwater to go astern into the berth at Gare Maritime, we were met by gunfire from German tanks on the hill road leading to Wimereux. With both turbines turning as fast as they had ever done, I recall looking through a porthole to see a man perched astride the light standard on the ten-minute whistle buoy – whither he had arrived by small boat – waving frantically. To pick him up would, I suppose, have placed the ship in immediate danger of being sunk, and so he had to be left behind, most probably to be taken prisoner.

Returning to Dover, we lay again at the eastern arm and, as time passed, the news grew more serious. The Germans had occupied Boulogne and Calais was being held only by a desperate rearguard action. Then came the expected order for evacuation; all available ships to proceed to Dunkirk. I well remember the weather which was nothing less than perfect for such an operation. Hot, still days with a brazen sun shining through the haze over a placid, almost oily sea. From the French coast could be heard sporadic explosions and the ominous rumble of gunfire increasing in intensity as each day went by. The enemy was fast closing in on Dunkirk and with the route along the coast past Gravelines no longer available, our course was circuitous to the westward. From this time onward I was acting Chief Engineer, preoccupied with fuelling and plagued by a main generator defect caused no doubt by age and additional load imposed by current for D.G. coil. This left us with only the port generator to carry all the electrical equipment, and gave rise to some anxious moments, considering that failure to keep the D.G. coils in operation would have left the ship particularly vulnerable to magnetic mines.

On one occasion, I came on deck for a breath of fresh air (the temperature of the manoeuvring platform during those sultry days hovered around an uncomfortable 100/120 degrees F.) to see a ship immediately ahead lurch violently to starboard on a boiling creamy brown mountain of water. She had probably detonated an acoustic mine, then a new product of devilish ingenuity which allowed perhaps two ships to pass over without harm but exploded under the third. I was transfixed by this sight and thought "there, but for the grace of God, goes *The Maid of Orleans.*"

Circulating water for the condensers was another trouble. Going in close to the beaches with the fore foot almost tapping the sand, or lying alongside the moles where ships had not lain before, there was at times very little water under the ship and to keep the tubes clear of mud and water presented no small problem.

The harbour and port of Dunkirk made a depressing sight. Burning oil tanks and dense clouds of smoke spread a pall of gloom, which to some extent prevented exact detection by hostile aircraft and gave some cover to those sorely in need of it. A considerable number of wrecks in the vicinity and approaches made navigation a nightmare. All this came as a profound shock to those of us who had previously been engaged in trooping from Southampton to Cherbourg in orderly conveys with no more excitement than an occasional U-boat or E-boat scare or a German plane reconnaissance. To see a company of guards form up and march along the quay at Cherbourg, tall and erect, though inspiring, gave little indication of what was to follow. Here was a real shooting war in which merchant seamen suddenly found themselves in the armed services, but the armament of *The Maid of Orleans* consisted only of a few Lewis guns and a 12 pounder.

To my mind, the miracle of Dunkirk, as it is called, was the still weather and calm sea which made the operation possible. While one might expect good weather during the summer months, it cannot be counted upon, and any swell would have made an inshore approach extremely hazardous. Towards the end, a strong northerly wind caused a rather rough sea but, in the main conditions were extremely good and enabled us to make six trips, lifting in all 5,319 men from the beaches.

I have no personal recollection of any ordered routine, such as meals and sleep, apart from dozing uneasily over the mess-room table. Impressions remaining with me are of a merciful providence allowing this operation to be successful by what I thought was phenomenally calm weather, of soldiers utterly weary and unwashed who, in their withdrawal, showed no haste and took each his turn in an orderly queue evincing a cheerfulness at which I marvelled. Lying alongside the east mole, we embarked troops who came in a slow procession negotiating the gaps caused by bombing and artillery fire, and bridged by narrow, makeshift gangways. They brought their wounded with them, patiently and without panic. By now the German had the inshore end of the mole well within range and embarkation seemed painfully slow.

Little incidents struck me as remarkable, some even funny.

Loading large cases of ordnance maps for Dunkirk when it seemed clear that the only maps of any use would have been charts indicating the position of wrecks in the approaches. A naval commander in immaculate uniform directing soldiers down a precarious gangway, his white shirt cuffs shining incongruously through the smoke and gloom of the evening. A Second Lieutenant, safely aboard with very good prospects of getting back to England, finding time to worry about the loss of a swagger cane. French troops squatting against a wall on the sun-baked Admiralty Pier at Dover nursing, as it seemed, their ancient, single-loading rifles. Thousands of rounds of .303 ammunition an inch or two deep on the shelter deck, and the unprecedented sight of destroyers and cross-channel ships two and three abreast in Dover Harbour.

I think the majority of us were puzzled as to why Hitler did not follow up this apparent rout, for Dover and South-East England seemed critically vulnerable, and most people concerned in the operation felt that an appalling catastrophe had occurred. Yet, curiously enough, it was sometime afterwards that it came to me as a surprise that, during the evacuation, I had never heard anyone speak openly of defeat.'

Later, James went to see his father after his mother received word that they might be able to see him briefly if they went to what was then known as the eastern arm at Dover – he says, "Mother took me with her, I remember it was a heavy, overcast afternoon as we made our way along the seafront. The Harbour was full of ships and there were muffled explosions and columns of black smoke rising on the other side of the channel. The ominous atmosphere must have made an impression on me. The policeman on the dock gate told us that there was no possibility of seeing anyone, so our journey had been in vain, and as we returned, householders were standing at their gates, and one said – 'this town will be raided before the nights out.' When my father did eventually arrive home, he fell on the bed and slept for 15 hours.

Before Dunkirk was over it must have been decided that mother and I would go to stay with relations in Brighton. While we were waiting at Folkestone Central Station, troop trains kept rumbling through. The troops seemed to be in good spirits and were leaning out of the windows, laughing and shouting, and throwing their French coins onto the platform. After a long wait we boarded a train already full of servicemen, some wearing blood stained bandages, some delirious and nurses were going up and down the aisles, tending them. It was after midnight by the time we reached Brighton."

One member of the B.E.F. who came back on one of the journeys made by the *Maid of Orleans* was Alan Scobie of 211th Field Pack Company, 44th Division Royal Engineers. He says, "when the retreat was in full swing and it was – "Every man for himself," we started the march back towards the coast and the Sergeant Major pointed out the exact road we had to take for Dunkirk. A few minutes after we started on the march, this route was attacked by Stuka dive-bombers – so we scattered. Afterwards we continued the march, or walk as it now was, back towards the coast. We found that on either side of this road there were many army vehicles that had been abandoned – one of these was full of ammunition, which exploded with a gigantic roar soon after we'd passed it. We walked for a day and a night, eventually arriving on the beaches to the west of Dunkirk. On the way I discovered a tin of plums on the ground which I managed to open with my bayonet, a friend of mine shared this treat with me – it was the first we had eaten for two days.

I spent a full day on the beach and eventually was taken on board the pleasure steamer, *Maid of Orleans* – I went to sleep straight away and didn't wake up until after we had arrived at Dover."

Back on the beaches of Dunkirk, on the 29th May, Captain Tennant and his men were doing a solid job in a situation that was becoming increasingly more difficult, with the constant arrivals of more troops from all over the place. He was still in touch with Dover of course, so they were aware of the situation there, with Ramsay still desperately trying for more destroyers. Amongst the destroyers that had gone to Dunkirk after the order had gone out on the 27th May for all available destroyers to head for that port, were the *Jaguar*, the *Anthony* and the *Malcolm*. A sailor on the *Jaguar* reported that on approaching a nice sandy stretch of beach, just over a mile away, suddenly, what looked like vegetation growing near the foreshore, came to life – what had looked like shrubbery had materialised as men.

Despite the fact that the destroyers had at first been sent to give covering fire for the merchant ships, transports, tugs and steamers, they now sent in their own ships boats to pick up troops. This was a slow, laborious job. Other destroyers were doing the same, and were also still shelling the enemy positions.

By May 29th several of the destroyers had been damaged by enemy fire. Reported sunk were the *Grenade, Grafton* and *Wakeful*. One of the troops, who was lucky not to have been on either of the

80

last two mentioned, is Ernest Oakland of Nottingham. He had joined The Royal Engineers at Chatham early in 1940. At the time of Dunkirk he had been married for fifteen months with a baby son born in October 1939.

Within a month of joining, Ernest had been sent to France – helping to build landing strips for the R.A.F. After the German Blitzkrieg had begun on May 10th they were ordered to go to Belgium. After the retreat from there, he eventually found himself on the beaches of Dunkirk. He was there for thirty six hours; after this, with some others, he was taken by a rowing boat to *H.M.S. Grafton*, but as they climbed aboard an officer came along and ordered them off again, saying the ship was overloaded. They went back down the scrambling nets and into the dinghy, and were taken over to another destroyer – which turned out to be *H.M.S. Wakeful*. Once more they were sent away – this time finishing up on *H.M.S. Vivacious*, and once on board felt "home and dry" even though the ship was vibrating with all the gunfire against the diving Stuka's.

The *Grafton* and *Wakeful* were both sunk that evening – they sunk within a few minutes of being hit. All this happened on the 29th May.

Ernest says, "I got to Dover about midnight and was put on a train which eventually ended up at a station somewhere near Salisbury Plains. We stayed here until they got us sorted out – our unit was scattered all over England."

Because of all the losses, The Admiralty had decided to withdraw the most modern of the destroyers under Ramsay's command, leaving him with just the older ones – a bitter blow! The order couldn't have come at a worse time; soon however, these were returned to him after he had reluctantly agreed to only send them to Dunkirk under the cover of dark.

Also at Dover, they were getting first hand reports as to what it was like retreating from the enemy to the beaches. One soldier told how he had marched with a machine-gun bullet in his foot for several days; another described how British artillery put up a barrage a mile long in one section – "the Germans just advanced right into it," he said, "their casualties must have been tremendous. More and more men were thrown into the fight and they came on relentlessly."

One infantry man who had not eaten for days, said – "Fleeing refugees hampered our movements all the time. The Germans spared neither man, woman or child. They were mown down by the great German war machines which came on – wave after wave. They stopped for no one. It was mass murder at its worst!"

For Noel Eyley, an early Militia man, the seriousness of the position became more apparent after listening to a wireless report from London. He was in the R.A.S.C. and assigned to the Corps H.Q. On the retreat, after they had had to destroy the transport that they were on, they joined the endless stream of troops that were heading towards Dunkirk. He remembers seeing a Grenadier Guards captain, smart and disciplined, sorting out anyone who looked slovenly – "March you, march, hold your heads high." Meanwhile, at the other side of the road, a file of infantry men – probably from the Green Howards, walked grimly on in the opposite direction, destined for the ever-nearing front in an effort to storm the advance. He thought, 'How many won't return?'

Noel carries on in his letter to me. "Before entering Dunkirk, we paused for a while. In a deserted farmyard we found abandoned French mobile equipment, including a vat containing a small amount of coffee – tepid, dreg-laden and laced with some spirit or other. The French on the move, we concluded, had got their priorities about right! Never did coffee, even in that condition, taste so good as we scooped away with our mess tins to get some of the precious liquid. Revitalised we moved on, cautiously, for Dunkirk was ablaze."

Whilst they were on the beaches he remembers hearing the whine of a bomb falling nearby, and they quickly sought whatever cover they could – "I took the shelter of a broken down Bren carrier on my left." He says. "The thud came, the sand sprayed; the earth shook. After what seemed an eternity I raised my head cautiously. Was I still alive? – Yes – but the Bren-gun carrier was now on my right! Had it been hurled bodily over me – did I imagine it, or is my recollection at fault? I can never be sure; but the position of the bomb crater confirmed my suspicion at the time."

Later, when approaching the mole, they saw a young bearded Royal Naval officer, a lieutenant, acting as embarkation officer. He was unflinching and upright throughout – daunting and undaunted

82

by the havoc all around. The navy was there; all would be well for us. Especially when, scorning rank, he tore into a group of brasshats who tried to jump the queue by entering the head at an angle. "No-one, but no-one, goes along this mole without my say-so. Get to the rear and each of you collect fifty men first."

Noel goes on, "At last my turn came – coinciding with a canon firing attack. For protection I crouched under the concrete balustrade running the length of the mole. The man about three foot in front of me had his scull partly sliced away by a sliver of concrete – even as he reeled over and plopped into the water, his hand unconsciously, in death, clawed at his brain. The finality of it all lingers yet, sixty years on."

The first ship that Noel boarded was bombed and put out of action. The second one he boarded was on the other side of the mole. This got a few hundred yards out, was bombed amidships and fire broke out. He says, "I was thrown into the air midst engine-room debris, felt one leg snap like a twig and ended up completely trapped, apart from one arm free. The fire, and the instinct for self-preservation, drove me to claw myself out on deck. I don't remember how I got off that sloping deck – but I found myself in a rowing boat. A voice said – 'Here take the rudder corp. and steer for that ship over there while we row.' So I did.

Imagine climbing a rope ladder, one leg dangling uselessly; but it was the only way onto that merchantman. I found out later that the ship was fitted with depth charges. Once on board, helping hands made me as comfortable as possible down below, whilst we zig-zagged across the channel, dropping depth charges to deter some lurking enemy submarine. I lay there somewhere down below, feeling the ship quiver as the engines thrashed the prop shaft into life. 'What's this ships maximum speed?' I asked a young Merchant Navy officer.

'About fourteen knots.' Came the matter of fact reply, and a little later 'sixteen knots now.' – I could hear the vibrations increase. 'That's our navy,' I thought, Royal or Merchant; capable of doing the impossible when needed!"

Noel was put onto an ambulance train at Dover, and was eventually admitted to Seacroft Emergency Hospital in Leeds. He became quite a fixture there and was known to everybody as 'The Corporal.' The leg was slow to mend, after extensive surgery.

F.E. Lucas of Enfield in Middlesex has sent me the following account:

"I joined the Territorial Army, The Royal Corps of Signals at the Standard Telephone and Cables Limited, New Southgate, London in May 1939.

The company sponsored three signal sections of No.3 Company 44th Division. We all went to a camp at Dibgate, Folkestone in August 1939 for two weeks, during which we had a visit from the Princes Royal, who was Colonel in Chief of Royal Corps of Signals.

On Friday afternoon the 1st September 1939, we were called up and instructed to assemble at New Southgate in uniform and with all our kit. We were billeted in a house near the Company and on the evening of the 2nd September I was on stick guard at the main gate of the company (we were not issued with rifles) and it stormed that night. On Sunday 3rd September at 11.00hrs. war was declared and at 11.15hrs. the air raid sirens went off and we went into the air raid shelters. It was a false alarm.

The first line of the Signal section went to Tunbridge Wells and on the 7th September the 2nd line, 12th Division went to the tennis club ground at Chiswick. Here we did our training in morse code, office routines, parade ground duties and trench digging.

In December I was posted to Crewkerne, to E section, no 2 Company, 44th Division, and was billeted behind the White Hart pub. The officer commanding was Lt. Withers, who we nicknamed 'Queenie'.

Christmas dinner, which the local people had arranged, was eaten in the Corn Exchange. We went on leave for the New Year by train, which was specially booked.

The section I was in was attached to the 57th Field Regiment RA, who were billeted in the village of Stoke Sub Hamdon, near Crewkerne, and in February we joined the Regiment for Manoeuvres on Salisbury Plain. It was very cold when we started off from Stoke Sub Hamdon travelling in impressed vehicles as we had not been kitted out with army vehicles. It turned milder during those days on Salisbury Plain and the ground turned to mud and chalk. On March 30th we

84

eventually entrained to Southampton and went to Cherbourg during the night on the LNER boat.

Rations were handed out, a tin of MacConochie's Meat and Veg. And a packet of hard biscuits. Sleep was impossible. On arrival at Cherbourg we entrained to somewhere in mid France; we travelled on a French train which had hard wooden seats. We had to march in free kit to another village, where our transport met us. We then motored up through France till we reached Merville, not far from the Belgium border. We were billeted in the dance hall behind the café.

On the 10th May the Germans attacked Belgium and the airfield near Merville was bombed. We all got dressed with tin helmets and gas masks etc. That evening we all left Merville and the 57th Field Regiment went into Belgium. Eventually the guns were dug-in and the Signals were with the RHQ in a small Belgian farmhouse – all the civilians had gone. The Division was in the 3rd Corps, and we were near Oudermande. On the 22nd or 23rd May, the Germans advanced and the Regiments' guns started to fire. After about two days, we had a message by phone to say that we were surrounded (I believe it was the Fifth Column.) The rest of RHQ had to stand by all night. When we got the call, the Regimental CO threatened us with his revolver not to retreat.

The night before, a tracked vehicle approached along the road. It was pitch black and our corporal, who had a Boyes rifle (0.500 Bullets) shouted out, "Stop, who goes there?" – No reply; so the corporal fired. The tracked vehicle was a British Bren Gun Carrier, and was stopped with a bullet through the radiator. The driver was not injured.

Some twenty clerks and signals were detailed to go forward to stop the Germans. Myself with five others and the signals officer had to go across the fields to guard a 4-gun troop position. The gunners had gone; they had left all their guns in position, but had not made them inoperative by removing the breech blocks and firing pins etc. The orderly officer was ordered to go back to the transport lines and fetch the gun tugs, but we never saw him come back. We seven stayed at the gun position till nightfall and went back through the fields until we reached a barn, we all went to sleep there until morning.

The following day we marched back through the Belgian lines and villages till we got to a convent where the nuns invited us to stay the night.

We slept on tiled floors, fully dressed. The next morning we had a breakfast of eggs, bread and butter and coffee. While we were eating the Germans fired a shot at the church tower, which certainly shook the villagers. After breakfast we carried on marching till we came to the Divisional RASC supply column. We got a lorry back to the Regiment, which was sited in a big field, the lorries had also arrived. We found out that the seven of us had been posted missing.

It was now the morning of the 29th May. The Regiment was ordered back to Dunkirk. We were now travelling in our vehicles. At one point on our journey the lorry was ordered to make a dash through a junction which the Germans had in gun range and were shelling. I was laying down on the back of the lorry. We got through safely.

We arrived at a field just outside Dunkirk which was nearly full of all sorts of army vehicles. The drivers were instructed to dump the trucks and destroy the engines. The engine oil was let out of the sump and the engines run.

We then had to march back to Dunkirk – we went through the docks area. I saw many staff cars abandoned along the roads. These were stacked out with NAAFI rations: cigarettes and spirits. They were there for any soldier to help himself. I filled my water bottle up with rum.

I got down to the beach, which was all sand and soldiers. I remember a German plane coming over and spraying the beach with bullets and the soldiers digging for shelter in the sand. The oil tanks were ablaze and sending up thick smoke clouds. The ships, mostly destroyers, were alongside the wooden pier. They were firing against the German shore batteries – the Germans were firing back.

Late afternoon that day, I joined a crowd of soldiers along the embankment to the pier. Parts of the pier had been damaged by shells, and mess top tables had been placed for us to get along to the ships. I got onto the destroyer *H.M.S. Jaguar* and off we set. About half an hour later, three planes (ME 109's) bombed the ship. The ship's AA guns fired away. The ship had a near miss and many on

86

the top deck and bridge were killed by shrapnel – including the Regiments HQ Captain. The *Jaguar's* main steam pipe had been destroyed in the attack and the ship was stopped.

Another destroyer, *H.M.S. Express* came alongside and took us off (it already had a full complement of soldiers on board). At the same time, the Dutch skoot, *Rika*, already commandeered by the Royal Navy, came alongside and took off some 300 men from the *Express*, including myself. We sailed across the channel during the night to Dover.

In the early morning of 30th May, we entrained to Devizes, The HQ of the 1st Wiltshire Regiment. We were put in the barrack rooms and slept for quite a few hours. I remember writing a letter to my girl friend Kitty, and having to beg for a stamp – we had no English money and had not been paid.

After about four days we were sorted out and sent back to the 57th Field Regiment, who were being reformed in Kings Meadow, Oxford. Most of our kit had been left behind at Dunkirk, But I brought back my rifle and a complete bandoleer of .303 bullets. My greatcoat I gave to someone whilst on board the *Rika*, for warmth. All the members of the Signal section returned safely."

I should like to add a little more to this account – about *H.M.S. Jaguar*. She had been lying at the end of the mole, but just as she'd cast off and started heading for home, although there were no direct hits on her, the shrapnel had damaged her fuel tanks as well as the steam pipe; fortunately *H.M.S. Express* was close at hand. *Jaguar* had started drifting towards the shore, but the *Express* managed to tow her clear before taking the troops off, and the stricken ship then slowly returned to Dover.

On the beaches at Dunkirk and La Panne, confusion still reigned as troops were now arriving from 'everywhere.' One of these was Sgt. D. Tait of 248 Field Company, Royal Engineers (T.A.). He was called up a few days before war was declared – "Very young and itching to get at it." He said. "We had been taught to build a Bailey bridge and to blow things up, but not a lot more. So starting at the advance into Belgium as a sapper (having lost my stripes for 'borrowing' some pig potatoes from a French farmer to feed my squad on whilst they were building pillboxes.) We were very close to the Belgian/Dutch border, we bivouacked in a field near to some houses, and at dawn we were shelled by 88mm. Guns, some twenty shells landing amongst us – it was our first time under fire. There were some wounded and some fatalities. It appeared that our position had been passed on to Jerry by a French fifth columnist in a house nearby – he was dealt with later that day.

We then moved on to the defence line of the river Dyle, where, to our horror, we were put into slip trenches. Our knowledge of trench discipline was zero – sappers did not go into trenches – built them perhaps, but not to use them.

We had two days in these trenches and were learning to keep our heads down after a few shells had come our way. On the second night, we were relieved by the North Staffs. Who refused to use our trenches and set up home elsewhere – just as well, as the following day our old position received a pasting.

We started a strategic withdrawal through Louvain which was being heavily shelled. Because of the withdrawal, 'our roll of builders' was reversed to 'destroyers' and, supported by the infantry, we began to do as much damage as possible; blowing bridges, roads, culverts and railways. I remember that one man was given a 500cc Norton, with the panniers full of explosives, and told to do as much damage as he could – he enjoyed himself and was mentioned in despatches.

My main experience was helping to blow up one of the Boulevard bridges, north west if Lille, 100ft wide, it was an incredible and satisfying sight.

All the time we were retreating and as we went north, we began to see and feel that something was far from right. The days went by in a blur with little sleep, and food not always available. We began to see all sorts of wrecked transport along the roads. We saw perfectly good transport being wrecked by their drivers, some in tears, and with heavy hearts – destroying the engines. We were told to do the same, so we collected as much ammo and explosives as we could carry and then carried on, on foot.

On reaching La Panne, we were told to deploy ourselves in the sand dunes. To keep ourselves busy we explored the beach and the apartment buildings behind us for secure billets that night, and spent an uncomfortable night in a cellar. The next night we spent on the dunes and in the early hours of the morning, at first light, we noticed small boats approaching the beaches and taking men off to the larger transports laying further off. Some of these were getting badly knocked about by the Stukas.

After another night sleeping on the beaches, we were happy to meet up with some more of our comrades and together we continued to queue up for the small boats as they came inshore. The Stukas continued their attacks, and we would scatter when they approached – we were easy targets! We all gave a great cheer when, by concerted rifle fire, we were able to shoot down one Stuka – it made our day!

All this time the weather was marvellous, the sea warm, and under different circumstances it would have been enjoyable being there.

It became obvious that if the larger craft could get nearer to the beach, there could be a faster transfer of men. Our Lance Sergeant proposed that we, the R.E.'s, collect as much transport as there was on the beach, and at low tide push out the trucks as far as possible into the sea, thus creating a jetty. We had the very willing help of many men and soon there were larger boats coming in and filling up from this newly built 'pier.' It was heartening to see another jetty being assembled further along the beach. For this idea, and putting it into action, our Lance Sergeant was awarded the Military Medal.

That evening, we were taken off by a small cabin cruiser to the destroyer, *H M.S. Worcester* and landed at Dover."

With the call having gone out for more 'little ships' and the men to man them, the ports around the south east were a bustle of activity – the operation was now coming into full swing.

Back at home – in The Evening Argus, a headline said – 'GIVE US MORE AEROPLANES' – plea by B.E.F. men. After telling about troops arriving back in London, the article went on to say, '– The men told a reporter that the B.E.F. had inflicted casualties at the rate of at least five Germans to one British, and that everywhere our troops have demonstrated their fighting superiority, but the cry on the lips of everyman was – "for Gods sake give us more aeroplanes!"

After reading this, father said – "I really don't know what to make of this report – they make it sound as though we should be advancing, not retreating!"

By the time of The Battle of Britain we would know more of the answer to the question of where the R.A.F. were at this time, when, as at Dunkirk, and still heavily outnumbered – they would give a brilliant account of themselves!

Chapter Six

Journeys on Foot – Lifeboats

T he atmosphere at the ports around the south and south-east of the country was now electric, it was all systems go with the utmost speed – time was of the essence.

The organisation on the beaches at La Panne and Dunkirk was now beginning to make some sense, thanks to the Naval shore parties – but with more troops arriving all the time on the beaches, things were still chaotic.

However, even amongst all the devastation there were some things that remained as they were – as if nothing was happening, making the whole situation seem unreal. Bob Wrycraft of the 5th Battalion, Queens Own Royal West Kent Regiment, had reached the beach at Dunkirk in company with one good friend and a few 'sundry' others on the evening of May 29th.

Bob says, "After just a couple of hours sleep by the sea wall, and no immediate signs of being taken off, my friend and I decided to have a look around the town. The German bombs had created havoc and many lovely churches and other buildings were just a mass of rubble. How long we wandered around I have no idea, but eventually we decided to return to the beach. It was about 8 a.m. – the day had dawned warm and bright, and as we turned a corner from one road to another, there stood before us a row of two up, two down cottages. They were completely untouched by bombs and shells. Neat little front gardens with gates at the ends of the paths, leading to the front doors. We walked along this road in front of the cottages, and almost at the last one was an elderly gent sitting on a chair, smoking his pipe. We passed the time of day and gesturing to us, he invited us in. Well, it was immaculate, a lovely fire burning in the kitchen stove, with a kettle and a pot of coffee on the top.

A lady there, who we took to be his daughter, greeted us and invited us to sit down. She poured us a cup of coffee each, while the old gent produced two glasses of Cognac. All our other mates were on the beach and there we were living the life of Riley. It didn't last long, we realised we had to get back and thanking them with gestures and handshakes we bade our farewell. Our day had been made by two ordinary French people."

Bob, and the men with him, later joined a queue on the jetty and were taken to Folkestone on board *H.M.S. Vanquisher*.

When Belgium had surrendered and the retreat had begun, David Caple, who I mentioned had been on the convoy supplying materials for building the pillboxes on the Belgian border, had had an eventful journey before arriving at the beaches. He and two others had had to sleep in barns and fields and farmhouses on their journey. Sometimes they were successful in finding eggs in some of the deserted farm buildings. When they eventually arrived at the beaches, he remembers being told to go to a large white house standing back from the dunes where he would be issued with rations. He walked straight into a room that was full of the top brass of the army – "plenty of red tabs on the collars." He got a chit signed for supplies and quickly disappeared. This house had now become the General Headquarters of the army for all the personnel in that area. David, eventually made it safely back to Ramsgate. Also on the retreat from Belgium, Bombadier Philip Norburn of The Bedfordshire and Hearts Yeomanry, after his officer had been killed in a skirmish, found himself in charge of about twenty men. They were at Poperinghe and had just completed the task of blowing up an ammunition dump – they had also been ordered to blow up their trucks and 'sink' their artillery in the canals. After this it took a day and a night to get from Poperinghe to Dunkirk – "the whole thing happened so quickly," Philip told me. "It seemed like no time at all that back at Bethune, with no idea of this soon to happen, that we had been listening to Vera Lynn giving a concert at The Opera House there – I remember she sang Gounod's, 'Ave Maria' – the place was packed with troops and you could have heard a pin drop. I think this was before ENSA was formed."

92

Eventually, he somehow split up from his troops in the general confusion, and after spending some time on the beaches existing on the rations he had been supplied with, he was one of a group of men chosen by a naval officer to board one of the small boats that were now beginning to arrive on the scene a bit more frequently. Unfortunately the boat he got on was strafed by enemy aircraft and sunk, but being a strong swimmer he swam out to one of the destroyers about a further half a mile out to sea, and was picked up – he later arrived safely at Dover.

In July 1939, Jack Farley was called up for training in The First Militia, The Royal West Kents. He remembers that he and his fellow conscripts, apart from the battledress they wore, were measured up for an outfit consisting of grey flannel trousers, blue blazer, shirt and a red tie – they never got these outfits, events on the continent had something to do with that.

They did six months hard training at Maidstone Barracks. Here, Jack was something of an exception to the rule – he actually enjoyed it! After this, he and his Regiment did further training at Axminster. King George VI inspected them here, he shook hands with many of the men including Jack. The 'West Kents' then went to France. Jack had joined the signals section of the Regiment and was at their headquarters. Later, he had taken part in the counter attack on Arras, and also in a big battle at Oudinard. Eventually, with the collapse of Belgium, and when the general retreat was beginning, they had been given the order "Every man for himself," – and advised to try to make for the coast – aiming for a place called Dunkirk. Some of them, including Jack, managed to get some transport for some of the way – this was until the petrol ran out, and they had to destroy the trucks. They spent the next several days making their way on foot. They slept in barns and outhouses – there were quite a few empty houses on the route that they took, and slept in some of these as well. Jack says – "I remember coming across one house in particular where the kettle was still boiling on the cooker and a breakfast was ready laid on the table – everything left just like that, and the people gone!"

In the farm buildings they searched for eggs to supplement their meagre rations – sometimes successfully. At one time they came upon some abandoned trucks, and foraging in them, came upon a box containing some tins of peaches and Nestles milk – a luxury!

If they came to a pond, they would stop for a while and try to wash in it – although this wasn't exactly high on their priority. At one time they saw a large French gun being transported across fields in the general direction that they were going, so they hopped on. A bit later, after crossing a ploughed field – 'shaken and bruised' – they wished they hadn't.

On the way, some of the men decided to 'do their own thing,' and soon, there were just two of them – Jack and his friend Len Hayden, of the transport section. "Eventually, we got to the beaches – we couldn't see any ships at all, just a huge mass of men everywhere!" Jack told me.

The date was May 28th – it was early in the morning. For the next three days Jack and Len remained together on the beaches " – dodging the Stukas and trying to survive!" They spent quite a bit of the time they were there searching for food, but couldn't find any. "We were starving." Jack said. "We did come across a man on the sands brewing tea in a large old tin can – he had a total disregard for the Stukas and other enemy aircraft – he was a brave man. He gave us a cup of tea each, and to say that that went down well, is certainly something of an understatement!"

On the last day that they were there, they were directed by an officer to go to the jetty on the harbour. Jack says – "Just before dusk, a few of us, probably about twenty, got onto a boat that smelled very highly of fish; it was dusty and rusty and definitely foreign. It could have been a Dutch or Belgian trawler, I remember that the crew spoke in a foreign language. I don't remember much more about the crossing, because I was exhausted by then and went to sleep. Eventually, we found ourselves in Folkestone. We were helped by everyone when we got there – there were cups of tea, cakes, sandwiches and cheering words from people we had never seen before – they were patting us on our backs and asking if there was anything we wanted. Even the military police, the 'Redcaps,' were kind and helpful. It wasn't long however before we found ourselves on a train, which after about an hour moved off through the Kent countryside. I lived at Maidstone at the time and thought I was going home, but we eventually arrived at a barracks in Bristol, where we were kitted out afresh, and a couple of days later, went home on a week's leave. On asking Jack what has stuck in his memory the most of those days, in other words, what can he look back on and see most vividly – he told me – "without doubt, while we were on the jetty, looking across to the beaches and seeing all those men queuing up in the water, as far as the eye could see – just queuing and hoping that some boat would come and pick them up and take them home!"

Don Booker could have been amongst those that Jack had looked out on from the jetty; he was a dispatch rider with 228 Battery, 57th A/T Regiment RA 44th Division – he says:

"We were told to head for the coast – it was every man for himself. I was riding my 500 Norton motor cycle, but it ran out of fuel at Poperinge, so I dumped it and started to walk. I soon joined up with some other soldiers, and we eventually came across a farmhouse, where we found a table already for dinner – there was a cooked chicken on it, which we ate. Sadly, on looking outside we found what we assumed were the four occupants – they were dead. When we got to the beaches, by coincidence, I met a pal from my home town. He had a slight wound, but this was enough for him to board a hospital ship. I remember I called him a lucky devil but the ship he went on was bombed and blown up, and he was killed.

I spent two nights on the beach – scared stiff. Every time we were strafed I tried to bury my head in the sand – pointless of course, but a spur of the moment reaction. A Scotsman and myself decided to risk breaking ranks and head for an old rowing boat that we could see near the waters edge – there was only one oar though. An officer joined us and we managed to paddle it out to a large fishing trawler – it was foreign, with the crew all speaking in a foreign language. We went below deck where we stripped off our wet clothes. We were in the nude when we were told to get up on deck immediately as we were being transferred to the destroyer *Vivacious*. We grabbed the first clothes that came to hand, even if they weren't our own, and arrived on deck in quite a state. We were taken to Folkestone, where we received a marvellous reception from the ladies there. Later we boarded a train for Dorchester."

95

The destroyers laying off shore, needed more boats to ferry the troops from shore to ship – they would soon be forthcoming. Amongst those destroyers were the *Anthony* and the *Keith*, but it was clear to all of them on these ships that evacuating all the troops they could see on the beaches was, as one officer put it – "going to be like attempting to empty a swimming pool with a fountain pen!" The situation was desperate.

Harry Philcox, of the Shoreham Lifeboat – *The Rosa Woodd and Phyllis Lunn*, was sitting in the cinema when flashed on the screen came the words – 'Would Mr. Philcox report to the lifeboat station immediately.' He got there by 9.45 p.m. and by 10.00 p.m. he and the crew, coxed by Lenny Baker, were in the water and under orders to proceed straight to Dover; this was on the evening of 29th May. The Shoreham Lifeboat was just one of eighteen lifeboats that were called upon that day; another one of these was the Hastings lifeboat *The Cyril and Lilian Bishop*, coxed by George Moon. On arriving at Dover, there was quite a bit of waiting about – in other words waiting for orders from the navy. Harry told me, "With all the lifeboats there, you've never seen a better fleet of boats in your life!" It wasn't until 3 o'clock that afternoon, 30th May, that a launch arrived at where the crews had congregated; the commander on board this craft called for all the coxswains to gather around him. He told them that they wouldn't be required to take their lifeboats across – the navy were going to crew the boats. This order, as one can imagine, was received with very mixed feelings and caused much controversy. Afterwards – and to this day, there are still arguments about this. Some said some of the crews of the lifeboats didn't want to go, the fact is though that this was the order. Two lifeboats that were taken over by their own crews were the *Prudential* from Ramsgate and the *Lord Southborough* from Margate, they had received special orders from The Admiralty – but more of these two boats later.

Harry Philcox told me that many of the crewmen, including those from Shoreham and Hastings, went into the naval offices at Dover, asking why they couldn't crew their own boats, and were told that they were to be towed over under cover of darkness, and being towed over – several boats altogether – would make it more difficult to be detected by the German asdic.

That night, Harry and the other crew men returned to their homes, but the next day, 31st May many of them returned to Dover to see if they could help in any way – the word was that they were still looking for men to man some of the boats – Harry was one of those that were accepted. It turned out that they were shorthanded for an assortment of boats that were ready to go across to be used to ferry troops from the shore to the destroyers. They spent quite some time doing this – all the time under fire from the enemy. When it was all over they returned to Dover, crammed full of troops – Harry remembers that there were forty or fifty of them. Eventually, when all the lifeboats were back at Dover, they simply waited where they were until their crews arrived to collect them and take them back to their respective homes. Harry was joined by Coxswain Lenny Baker and other crew members and duly took the *Rosa Woodd and Phyllis Lunn* back to Shoreham.

I believe that the best description of the controversy concerning the lifeboats that didn't go over with their own crews is in Steve Peak's book 'Fishermen of Hastings.' Steve has given me permission to use this relevant piece from his book, and this includes an account of the Hastings lifeboat, the *Cyril and Lilian Bishop*, and includes some words from one of its crew.

'On May 30th , the Ministry of Shipping asked the R.N.L.I. to send as many lifeboats to Dover at once. The R.N.L.I. immediately ordered its 18 lifeboats stationed between Gorleston in Norfolk and Shoreham in Sussex, to put to sea. What happened next has been the cause of controversy ever since.

The first three lifeboats to arrive at Dover were from Hythe, Walmer and Dungeness. When their crews – some of whom held gallantry awards from the R.N.L.I. – heard what was expected of them they refused to go, apparently because they believed their vessels unsuitable for the task. The Navy ordered the three crews out of their boats, put in their own sailors and sent them across the channel. All the other lifeboats that arrived at Dover (except those from Ramsgate and Margate, which sailed to Dunkirk with their own crews) were then commandeered by the navy and their civilian crews sent home.

The confusion and emotion surrounding these incidents led to claims that the Hastings lifeboat crew may also have refused to go to

Dunkirk. At the time of writing, 45 years after the event, the only surviving member of the scratch crew that took the *Cyril and Lilian Bishop* to Dover was Bill Terrell. He recalled what happened on that day: 'We'd been off fishing during the night, so when we came home early in the morning we went home to bed. When we got up later in the morning and went down to the beach all the other boats were off. I said to my brother "Someone must have had a good catch!" After a while we found that they had all gone to Dover.

'After dinner we went down to the beach again and George Moon came running along, saying "I've had orders to take the lifeboat to Dover – will you make up the crew?" Me and my brothers Jim and Ted said yes. The only three regular members of the crew on the trip were George Moon the coxswain, Bill Hilder the mechanic and Will Martin the second mechanic. The others that came were 'Bodger' Barton, 'Jumbo' White and Fred Button. We left Hastings beach near enough 4 p.m. that afternoon. All boats had to be in the harbour by sunset, otherwise they'd be fired on, and where it was getting dark when we were off Folkestone we put in there. We slept the night on the floor of the Seamen's Mission.

Next morning we got up about 5am, went along the café, had a bit of breakfast, went back to the lifeboat and proceeded to Dover. When we got there we went to the Admiralty survey boat that was giving orders. They told George Moon we'd have to go across from one buoy to another to avoid the mines. He asked if we could have a machine gun on the foredeck – they said no. He said can we have a rifle – they said no, all you can do is go to the Prince of Wales Pier, load up with petrol and get what food you want.

'So we went to the pier and got out of the boat, I don't know where the others went, but George Moon went to see about the petrol and Bill Hilder and myself walked along the parade and then came back. Then we saw two sailors in the lifeboat. Bill got wild and shouted "What are you doing in there?" They said "All we want to do is start this engine." George then said that all the lifeboats had been commandeered by the Navy – we had to get railway warrants and come home. The boat had just been painted up. When she came back to Hastings they found sand in her forward locker and in her masthead light, so she might have capsized.'

The *Cyril and Lilian Bishop* also returned from Dunkirk with a hole in her bow, and it was clear from her general condition that she had been well used at Dunkirk. She probably lay just offshore picking up swimmers and transferring them to larger vessels in deeper water. Just how many soldiers the *Cyril and Lilian Bishop* and most of the other lifeboats saved is not known, but the Ramsgate and Margate lifeboats rescued an average of 850 a day each. It is believed that the *Cyril and Lilian Bishop* was at Dunkirk at least over the weekend of June 1st and 2nd; her regular crew brought her back from Dover to Hastings on June 5th.

Back in France, it wouldn't be long before General Gort would be transferred back to England – reluctantly! Churchill had ordered him to return, and he eventually got back on June 1st after a huge muddle in orders, which resulted in his being transferred to and from various ships, including *H.M.S. Grebe* and *H.M.S. Keith*. General Alexander replaced Gort in command of the B.E.F.

On the beaches, the hellish attacks by the Stukas and other aeroplanes, continued – as did the numbers of troops arriving there. By this time there were more loud enquiries about where the R.A.F. were – they were sighted now and again, but nowhere near as often as the Luftwaffe in its persistent raids.

The facts are, that the R.A.F. fighters, which were heavily outnumbered by their German counterparts, did cover the beaches from first to last light each day, but resources were so short that only three or four squadrons could be airborne at one time; that is to cover all the approaches of the Luftwaffe to the beaches, and hopefully, attacking them before they got there.

92 Squadron, led by the renowned Robert Stanford Tuck, usually took off with perhaps twelve or fourteen aircraft each time, but taking into consideration damage and malfunctioning, this was sometimes as low as six. Tuck and the other members of 92 Squadron flew to Dunkirk on nearly every day of the evacuation. In Larry Forrester's book about Bob Tuck – 'Fly For Your Life' it includes the following statistical piece:

'The Air Council reckoned they'd taken the first round. In nine days over the Dunkirk area – from May 26th to June 3rd – at least

377 enemy aircraft had been destroyed for a loss of 87 R.A.F. machines. Exactly four and one third for every plane expended – or, since the majority of enemy machines were multi-engined type carrying crews, about nine dead or captured German airmen for every British fighter pilot who did not return.'

One other thing that Larry Forrester also points out in his book, is about the state of tiredness of the fighter pilots already in France, especially in the days just before Dunkirk. The Luftwaffe's policy in fighting the Hurricane Squadrons (the Hurricanes were mainly in France – Air Marshall Dowding kept the Spitfires for the home bases) had been to overwork the British pilots, to keep them in the air until they were exhausted and could fight no more. (One Hurricane pilot, Geoffrey Allard, was actually lifted from his cockpit at the end of a day's fighting, fast asleep) – and these men had to fly with precision and accuracy; at least we were now gaining in experience in time for the eventful and critical period soon to come – The Battle of Britain!

One of the large numbers of the men of the B.E.F. now arriving on the beaches, was George Fox of the 238 Field Company, 1st Division, Royal Engineers. This company had been responsible for blowing up 60 bridges during the retreat.

George says, "On the morning of Wednesday 29th May we were about to detonate one of the smaller bridges, when our section officer ordered some of us to make our way to where we could see a huge pall of black smoke – 'that's Dunkirk!' He said.

Later the same day, whilst on the beaches, some folding boats were brought to us. There was a minesweeper out about a 100 yards from the beach. A soldier tied a rope around himself and swam out to this minesweeper, where the crew tied it to the ships railings. We had tied the other end to a large stake driven deeply and firmly into the sand. These folding boats could take about forty men standing – the idea was to haul themselves along the rope to the waiting ship. Sadly nobody brought the first boat back, and it drifted out to sea. When the second boat was full, an officer drew his revolver telling two men to bring it back – or else!

He also told them that they would be able to stay on the next boat, which was the one that I went on.

100

That evening, we left the French coast; I remember being given cocoa and a cheese sandwich and then falling asleep – I woke up in Dover.

Fusilier Norman Prior was a Militia man serving with the 5th Battalion the Lancashire Fusiliers, which formed part of 125th Brigade. They had been part of the B.E.F. line along the river Escaut after the German advance had begun. Norman says, "We were told to be ready for a special task one morning; a little over an hour later we were sent to cover the withdrawal of the 6th Lancashire Fusiliers who had been defending the old fortress town of Tournai. When we saw them coming through – many of them wounded and with field dressings and bandages, and all looking exhausted – we wondered what chance we had. We were twenty nine men and one officer. They had been a battalion."

Hours later, the job done, they too withdrew, crossing a bridge on the way and being roundly cussed by a demolition party of Royal Engineers who had been waiting for hours to blow up the bridge.

At Seclin, Norman's section was positioned in a cotton mill, where, despite shelling, bombing, machine gun attacks and the resulting fires, the owner flatly refused to allow the troops to smoke!

Food was still a problem, "as a detached unit we belonged to no-one and everyone was on half rations anyway so there was none to spare for us. We sent Charlie Layland into the town to see what he could raise. He went off at 10.30 in the morning, when he hadn't returned by 6.30 that evening we were ready to write him off. Then in he came with two large brand new black shopping bags. One was full of food, cheese and biscuits and things, the other was packed with bundles of 100 Franc notes, some place had been blown open, he said. We shared the money and food in that order."

When the Bren Carriers and their crews moved on they found they were completely on their own. A brief encounter with enemy tanks was avoided when they discovered that their one anti-tank weapon, a Boyes AT rifle, had suffered a bent barrel and was useless.

At a cross roads they faced the problem of breaking into a stream of traffic, both military and civilian. A helpful British Redcap used his revolver to suggest to a French officer driving a civvy car that he stop and let the carriers in.

The road was under constant attack from the air and the chaos grew worse as vehicles were wrecked – one carrier was forced off the road and a track torn off – or ran out of fuel. The carrier syphoned petrol from abandoned wrecks to keep going.

Sixteen miles from Dunkirk, Norman's group were down to two carriers – a gradual twenty foot drop from the road into the field alongside helped them skirt round a major blockage, but their progress came to a final halt when they struck the wide canal, and the only remaining bridge was a narrow footbridge.

"We decided with regret to destroy the carriers and split up into twos to make our way to Dunkirk. We must have looked like a pair of waifs and strays when we met an NCO along the road. He directed us to La Panne and the beaches.

Even when we saw the ships lying off and being bombed from the air I still had no idea they were there to take us home. I really believed they were going to take us elsewhere along the coast to continue fighting.

Our next job was filling sand bags to serve as ballast in the lorries which had been driven into the sea to form a sort of pier for the rescue boats. Later, exhausted and soaking wet, he found himself helping to push overladen collapsible boats out to deeper water, until they floated.

"By the next night things were quieter, people were wondering off to find cellars or sheds, to sleep. Then a boat came in and the word came to get the collapsible boats loaded. We mustered about ten or a dozen off the beach and it was decided that it was now our turn to go.

I got in last and found myself in the back with an oar. That meant that I would have to row back. Next time I managed to be one of the first on board, there were only about seven of us by then. We were taken aboard the minesweeper *Halcyon* where we took our wet clothes to the drying room and the crew gave us blankets and mugs of hot cocoa. Four hours later we were in Dover."

Tommy Sands, of the 66th/(Leeds Rifles) Anti Aircraft Regiment, R.A. was making concrete bases for the guns to fire from, when a dispatch rider suddenly appeared and told them to stop what they were doing and make their way to Dunkirk. It was agreed by the officers and N.C.O's that they should separate into small parties and make their own ways. The route that Tommy and his group picked was a round about one, going either past or through, Douai, St. Pol, Bethune, St. Omer and Ypres. All these places had been bombed, the roads were filled with refugees – old men, women, children and babies – they carried what possessions they could on old carts or prams; it was a pitiful sight.

Tommy and the men with him had to search for whatever food they could – which was very little; they were lucky on just one occasion when they found some eggs at a derelict farm. After a long walk they made it to the beaches, and were eventually taken out to a destroyer – *H.M.S. Codrington*. Tommy can only remember climbing up the scramble net – how he got there is a blank, but, what he can remember, because he is small of stature, a large bearded sailor leaned over the side of the ship, grabbed him by his waist belt, and called to one of his mates "Shall I throw this one back – he's only a little one!" They didn't.

After being well received back in Blighty, Tommy carried on with the war

Lance Bombadier Gerald Johnson, of 51/54 Battery, 10th Field Regiment, R.A. With a couple of friends of his arrived on the beaches by means of a very different sort of transport to nearly everyone else.

In his letter to me Gerald says, "After seeing action in Belgium, my friend Sergeant Sam Woods (Later to be my best man.) and Signaller Basil Johnson, a 'Brumie' and no relation, and myself had been split up from the rest of our group, and we were heading towards the coast. On the way, a chunk of shrapnel tore a gaping hole in the petrol tank of our transport. Wearily, we set out on foot. I was still carrying my pack, plus my rifle and to make matters worse, it was very warm. After only two or three miles we began to feel the effect. Then our pace quickened as an idea came to us. We had spotted a group of French/Moroccan soldiers lounging about, with horses nearby. After a hurried consultation between ourselves, and noticing that the soldiers didn't seem to be bothering much about their horses, we grabbed three of them and mounted them. As we had no idea of 'exactly' where we were going, we followed the streams of exhausted and downcast troops who were all heading in the same direction – 'surely they couldn't all be wrong!'

103

We rode the horses for ten miles before arriving just outside Dunkirk. We stopped by a field and left the horses there – a friendly slap on their rumps, and we bade them goodbye.

For almost two days we huddled on the beach and found ourselves moving towards the mole, miraculously surviving the Stukas, the bombing and the strafing. Then, by megaphone, regulars and reservists were told to get together in bunches of fifty and approach the mole. There we marched out to the farther of two destroyers moored alongside. Thus we came to Dover.

At Dover, Ramsay had decided that Captain Tennant, at Dunkirk, urgently needed some assistance in getting the troops off the beaches and onto what boats were available – with a 15 mile stretch of beach to cover, he and his officers and men were facing a daunting task. Ramsay decided to send Rear Admiral Wake-Walker, with two commanders, to take over command of everything afloat off the shore of Dunkirk.

To start with, Wake-Walker directed operations on board *H.M.S. Keith*, but he soon became a familiar sight patrolling just off the beaches in an M.T.B.

Life on board the destroyers that were now receiving the troops from the little ships, was not only hazardous, but also becoming frantically busy.

Frank Brookshaw, who was an ordinary seaman aboard *H.M.S. Anthony* at the time of Dunkirk, described some of what took place to me:

"Our armaments were 4 x 4.7 inch low angled guns, torpedoes, and two twin Lewis guns. The ammunition pads on the Lewis guns had to be changed daily because the salt from the sea spray starting to corrode the cartridge cases, which caused jamming. These guns were mounted outside the wheel-house on the lower bridge – only useful if being strafed or aimed at the lower point of an aircraft making a dive bombing attack – usually a Junkers 87 (Stuka).

Once we had started the evacuation, our captain, Lt. Commander Thew – nicknamed 'Pugs' by the crew, commandeered six of the Bren guns from the army aboard the ship, and mounted four of these – the most reliable ones; but our anti-aircraft defence was negligible while operating off the beaches. The captain relied on speed when being attacked by a Junkers 87 – waiting to see when the bombs were released, then either going hard to port or hard to starboard. We were lucky, but did have one near miss resulting in some damage – there were no casualties. The Naval report shows that this was on May 30th.

To enable the ship to make these port or starboard turns at high speed, it was necessary to put all the troops below decks as we took them aboard, or they might be washed overboard.

On our first day there, as we approached the French coast, we could see the black smoke from the ships burning in Dunkirk Harbour, amongst them was a hospital ship. We could see the troops on the beaches – like swarms of ants – it looked to be an impossible job!

We did not anchor, although we went in as close as the tide would permit, and then just idled, in order to enable the small craft to come alongside. When the troops were on board, we gave them hot tea, bread and bully beef; we dried their clothing and gave them such first aid as we could – we did not carry a doctor.

Whilst this was going on and we were still picking up troops, if the enemy attacked we had to increase speed and steam out to deeper water and then return when they had gone – this, of course, slowed down the evacuation.

We worked mainly in the La Panne area, but did make one trip into the harbour. We noticed that the mole had been holed in several places, but the naval beach parties had made repairs where possible. We went in stern first – it was low tide and to get the troops on at a faster rate, we got mess tables up onto the deck and wedged them to the mole, and got the troops to slide down them. Fortunately the weather was quite good during all of this. When we had taken on as many as we could, we would make for Dover, unload, then off again after cleaning all the mess off the ship.

I have often thought what an opportunity the Luftwaffe had missed by not bombing the harbour at Dover whilst the destroyers were unloading hundreds of troops and then collecting more stores.

My job during the whole operation was in the wheel-house, the coxswain took over the wheel and I stood alongside him transmitting the engine revolutions by telegraph to the engine room, by turning a wheel after the coxswain had repeated the order from the skipper via a voice pipe from the bridge – the engine room then acknowledged this. It was quite a tense moment during a bombing attack, waiting for the skipper to pass the order in order to give the order – either hard to port or hard to starboard, and then to feel the '*Anthony*' reacting to the order and getting out of trouble yet again! The bridge was wide open – no cover. The skipper, other officers, lookouts and signalmen were all exposed to the elements.

There is more about Frank Brookshaw in the epilogue.

Amongst those still arriving on the beaches was Douglas Gulland, of The Royal Engineers. He had been in a section defending the Escaut Canal when the big retreat had started. He and his section spent the next several days sometimes in transport, but mainly walking to Dunkirk, it was hard going, especially as they had had no food for quite some time. When they arrived in the town of Dunkirk, they found a N.A.A.F.I. wagon that had been put out of action by the bombing – it was still full of sweets, so they took what they could carry and lived off these for the next few days whilst they were on the beaches awaiting a boat to take them home.

All the time they were on the beaches, they were being dive bombed by Stukas using deep penetration bombs, which fortunately didn't explode until they were deep in the sand. Douglas told me that if they had been using scatter bombs – "I wouldn't have been here now, but the deep penetration bombs – even if you were standing close to where they penetrated – would have the effect of picking you up and hurling you several yards away, as it did in my case, but I was uninjured!"

On the third day there, they got on a frigate, which was subsequently bombed – a bomb went straight down the funnel – so they had to transfer to another ship, *H.M.S. Express* a minelaying destroyer. This eventually got them home.

Not only were many more troops arriving on the beaches all the time, but by now, to the relief of those on board the destroyers as well as the troops wading waist and even chest deep in the queues in the water – the little ships were beginning to arrive in greater numbers. They were quite an assortment – they were also a Godsend!

106

The Brighton Belle – Sad last moments
(Imperial War Museum – H.U. 3252)

Medway Queen – As a minsweeper

Troops on board Medway Queen

S.S. Maid of Orleans in W.W.1 camouflage as a troopship leaving Folkestone harbour where she was sent for some emergency repairs after a collision with a destroyer in Dover Harbour in May 1940 (via Mr. John Gilham).

"Help from the Red Cross"

Food in any language

"Service with a smile" – at Headcorn Station

"Sandwiches and souvenirs"

"Plenty of helping hands"

112

A pier of lorries left by British troops – Germans on the beach after the evacuation
(Imperial War Museum – H.U. 1860)

H.M.S. Vivacious alongside mole after an air attack – trawler sunk during the raid
(Imperial War Museum – H.U. 1149)

"Coming home on a Destroyer"
(Imperial War Museum – C 147)

115

Packed trains – plus a few photographers as well as helpers

Chapter Seven

The Journeys of Tigris I

One of the boats that Douglas Tough organised to go down river on 27th May was *Tigris I*, a former First World War submarine chaser, which had been converted by Tough Brothers as a passenger boat — mainly for summer pleasure cruises, carrying up to 350 passengers at a time.

Harry Hastings, the publican of the Gloucester Arms at Kingston and owner of *Tigris I* -after Douglas Tough had approached him, asked his sons Harry and Warren, both lightermen on the Thames, whether they would take the boat down river to wherever the Admiralty told them to — possibly as far as Southend or even Sheerness. They had agreed, and after they'd signed on an extra hand — fellow lighterman Bill Clark, offering him a days pay and the fare back home — they set off at seven o'clock on the morning of Monday 27th May 1940, on what would be a far more adventurous journey than they had been told to expect.

Some years ago, with Dunkirk still firmly in his mind, Bill Clark, the extra crewman, was being looked after by a nurse in an old people's home — this was towards the end of his life. Whilst she sat talking to him, he started to tell her a story about his time at Dunkirk and about the boat he went over there on — *Tigris I*. She listened intently to his story and decided it was important enough for her to write it all down — "so that it would live!" So, armed with pen and paper, she (over the weeks) got him to repeat everything to her, whilst she did her level best to write it down exactly as told. She made a good job of it, so, with a little editing where necessary — here is the story of *Tigris I* at the time of Dunkirk, as told to her by Bill Clark.

"I met Harry and Warren at seven o'clock sharp on Monday morning 27th May, at Kingston Gas Co. Wharf. I stepped aboard, had a good look round and everything seemed okay. A bit later, we were on passage to Southend where Harry had asked me to help get them to – they didn't know the waters that far down the river. At that time, all we knew was she was wanted by The Admiralty, and we thought that this was for evacuating kids out of London. I remember it was a bit chilly that the morning on the river – there was a bit of mist about. Just before we got to Teddington Lock, Harry brought me a cup of tea and told me that we had to go to Westminster Pier to see a navy bloke there for fresh orders. I said okay, but I'm not being messed about by any navy blokes; I told my wife that I'd be home this evening – probably between 10 and 11 o'clock, if all went well.'

On the way down river, we washed the decks down and cleaned the brass, eventually arriving at Westminster Pier at 09.50 – not bad going from Kingston! We went alongside the pier, where we called out – 'Pier Ahoy.' A bloke came out, he was wearing a uniform – plenty of gold braid on his sleeves and scrambled egg on his hat.

'What do you want,' he said. 'We've got no berths here for you!'

I said – '*Tigris I* reporting for orders sir.' – Giving him all the old bull. By then half the navy had shown up, officers and ratings. I thought we were going to be put under arrest. The scrambled egg bloke said 'Proceed at once to Gravesend Pier and report. So once again we were on our way down river. We got to Gravesend Pier at about 1 p.m. I stepped onto the pier, where a P.O. came up to me and said 'What do you want here?' I told him that I didn't know and that we'd come there for orders. He took me to see the chief officer there, who, after he'd filled in some papers with our details, said, 'you'll want rations for three days for you and your crew.'

I said, 'three days? – I'm hoping to be back home by tonight!'

He said, 'you'll still need stores for three days, and whether you and your mates remain as crew or not, the boat will still need stores!'

I went back to the others and told them about the stores. Harry said 'Good, make sure you get plenty – anything left, glad of it!'

We talked about all this for a while and I remember I said, 'there must be something big on, do you remember seeing all those ships'

118

lifeboats when we came by The Royal Albert Docks? A lock full of them – must have been over a hundred boats!'

After this I went off to the chandlers, where I knew the owner. His shop was about half a mile from the pier. 'What are you doing down here, Bill!' He said. 'There's definitely something big on isn't there – I've been rushed off my feet all morning!' I told him what bit I knew, and then gave him my list for the stores we wanted – I'd put everything on I could think of – eggs, bacon, cheese, meat, bread, candles, fags, matches, tobacco, cigarette papers ... the lot! I had to borrow a trolley to take it all back to the boat.

By the time I got back aboard, all the boat stores had arrived as well; petrol, paraffin, ropes etc. We were ready to sail for Southend once more – the time by now was 3.40 p.m., it was low water, we had lost two hours at Gravesend pier.

We were under way ten minutes later, and then, punching against the young flood, we had to find what slack we could. The small ships were coming up on the tide now, but it wouldn't be long before we'd see the 'big boys' – bound for Tilbury and the Royals – best to keep out of their way! No good going from one side of the river to the other to find slack, so we kept down the south shore on the port helm until we got to Coryton. We passed one of my firm's tugs, the 'Floesco,' off Coryton, running light for Brentford. He was well late on tide. We gave each other a shout as we passed They shouted 'Where are you bound?' I shouted back 'I don't know.'

We made Southend Pier at about eight o'clock that evening; it was chock-a-block with boats of all kinds. We went around inside the pier to find a berth – not a soul about to tell us anything, so we moored up to another craft. After this we got ourselves ready for the shore, a nice pint of beer and the train for home. We were just stepping ashore when a naval officer shows up with a big megaphone in his hand and shouted – 'All boats proceed to Sheerness.' There was no use arguing, we had to go! By this time there was activity on all the other boats – they must have been turned in when we had arrived. We were the last in, so we were the first to go.

We got over the water to Sheerness okay – two or three faster boats passed us on the way. When we got there we couldn't go in right away, they had to find berths for us. After about half an hour

119

though, we were berthed up. I said to the berthing master, a young P.O. – 'Any chance of getting a pint in your canteen before we go home mate?' He took us to the canteen there – I ordered pints for all of us. A bit later, after we had had a few pints, we had to go and see the captain. These naval establishments ashore are named after ships, and Sheerness was *H.M.S. Wildfire*. The captain stood up, introduced himself and we shook hands. He said, 'We want volunteers to take your boat to France.'

I said – 'What, that 'old cow' out there? She's as rotten as a pear! She's an old M.L. from the last war – No! Not bloody likely, not me.' The captain said that was okay and that he only wanted volunteers to evacuate the British force from Dunkirk. 'Dunkirk!' I said, 'Why didn't you say so before – yes, I'll go.' Harry and Warren immediately said they'd go as well.

After this the captain told us we'd have to sign papers for twenty eight days service in The Royal Navy. He asked, 'Who's the owner of the boat?' Harry told him his father was, and after a bit of wrangling about what the navy would have to pay us, and also after allocating most of this to our wives, the matter was settled – although I did argue that I wouldn't be paid less than the others – 'over my dead body!' I said. But this was soon cleared up as well. We then got permission to use his phone to contact our wives, telling them we'd be away for a while, but didn't know for how long. After this the P.O. took us to a big warehouse, and gave us some blankets, telling us to bed down there for the night – we were in the navy now! It was freezing cold laying on that floor and I didn't get much sleep. I remember thinking about getting those men back from France. The old *Tigris I* carried about 350 passengers – I thought that they'd probably put up to 400 on board her. I didn't fancy coming back across the channel like that.

Early the next morning I strolled down the quay to have a look at the old boat, and found some people aboard her – they were dock workers and shipwrights. I asked them what they were doing and was told that they had to put brown paper on all the saloon windows and paint all the brass work black or grey.

Later on, after waking the others, we went for breakfast. I noticed there were people everywhere – like flies! Hundreds of blokes flying about with all sorts of gear. When we got back on board we sat there watching them for a while. While we were talking and watching all that was going on, the captain, with a lieutenant (wavy navy) and two ratings came on board; they had small valises, respirators, macs folded over their arms and food for three days. The captain told us that these three were coming aboard as the rest of the crew, the lieutenant in charge. Knowing we'd be picking up men from the beaches, we had to take on more stores for them as well. We also took on board a couple of wooden ladders – each about eighteen foot long. 'What are these for – they'll be no bloody good, they'll float out from the side of the boat!' He didn't like my telling him this, but all he said was – 'You'll have to weight them with something.' We then went ashore again for the extra stores, and also gave in our civvy gas masks – we were given navy respirators and tin hats.

Later, after our new crew had been changed for another lieutenant with two ratings for some reason, we set sail for Dover. Outside, in the river, was a Fish Cutter armed with a couple of machine guns. She had three red lights up her mast in a triangle; we were told to follow her, but if we lost her we were to make our own way – and mind the minefields! We were soon under way and took up our position under the stern of our escort. We arrived off Dover at 16.00 hours on Tuesday 28th May – the weather was a bit blowy, the sea a bit choppy. We went down to the cabin for some grub and some shut-eye.

Just after ten o'clock that night we were called out and told to up anchor and follow the escort. By the time we got underway – all strung out, about six boats wide, *Tigris I* was in the head rank outside the starboard quarter of the Fish Cutter. We noticed that there were two destroyers accompanying us, one on each side of the boats – we were just one of many on the way to Dunkirk.

I had just finished my trick at the wheel, I'd been there for about a couple of hours when Harry came up and took over. I lent him my overcoat; I was the only one of us to bring one along. I went below and had an hour's doze – I couldn't sleep properly, I was too much on edge, I went back on deck. Our two destroyers had vanished – disappeared in the night! I had a good look round and could see, far ahead of us, to port and starboard, five big red glows – Dunkirk!

The petrol dumps were on fire; I called all the others on deck. It was just starting to get daylight, we could see the volumes of thick black smoke in the distance – the sea was very calm. Some of us went below and had a bit of breakfast – the last for a long time, but we weren't to know that.

We were at Dunkirk, and about to turn to starboard into the harbour, when bearing down on us was a hospital ship, all out for Blighty. Harry was at the wheel, belting ahead, I said 'Where are you going mate?' He said, 'Across her head.' I said 'You ain't you know – she'll cut us in half! Stop the boat and let her go, I bet he's given her a double ring and stopping for no one.' We stopped. The hospital ship went across our head at about twenty knots and the wash from the ship broke all over us. One big wave broke over the focsle head and washed *Tigris I* down from forward to aft – we were drenched from top to toe.

Soon, coming towards us at full tilt, was an M.T.B. flying an admirals pennant. Whether he was a full Admiral, half Admiral or what, I don't know. The lieutenant was on deck, and I had taken the wheel off Harry. A bloke on the M.T.B.with a megaphone shouted out 'Proceed to La Panne.'

As we were approaching La Panne, destroyers were coming towards us loaded with troops; you couldn't see any top hamper of the destroyers for men – they were everywhere they could get! Some were fully dressed, some were half dressed – they all waved to us. There was so much to see and to hear – away to starboard, hundreds – no thousands of men; some lined up in companies, there were columns and groups down to the waters edge. There were others, in the background, lying on the sand – some in the sand dunes. I had never seen such a gathering of people in all my life, not even at big football matches.

Ahead of us, a lot of noise was going on; it was the machine gunfire from the navy ships – the Germans were over the top of us, dropping bombs. A small ship was coming towards us, she was about four hundred tons, an old French tramp ship by the look of her. She was going all out – the bombs dropping all around her. 'She's had it!' I shouted out. 'No she ain't! – She's coming through the bomb splashes.' The splashes were as high as her wheel house. She came out of them like coming out of a fog – we gave her a big cheer, she

122

had got away with it! I called out – 'God, Harry boy, what have we let ourselves in for?' – Harry said 'I don't know mate! Coming out of civvy street into this lot – it makes you wonder if you're awake!' More bombs dropped near us, and the explosions rocked the boat. Machine guns were hard at it and A.A. guns were going off from the navy ships.

A fast navy launch came out to meet us. An officer gave us our orders for the day and wished us luck – we wished him the same. We had been told to go to some beaches about a mile further along and ferry as many troops as we could from there to some destroyers that were about a mile and a half off the shore. The sea was like a mill pond, not a ripple on it, and the sky as blue as blue could be – no wind whatever. We made for the shore; I believe we were the first boat on that part of the beach. It's worth noting here that we still had our sign-boards up on *Tigris I*, saying – 'This way to ladies toilet,' 'Gents toilet,' 'Watney's Pale Ale,' 'Guinness for strength,' 'Players,' 'Wills Woodbines' all these advertisements were still hanging about our boat.

We put our wooden ladders overside, one on each forequarter. We slowed down and then touched sand about 250 yards from the waters edge. The lieutenant started to give us orders as to what to do and how to do it. I said 'Aye, aye, sir, leave it to us , we'll make a good job of it!' I can't get it into my head I'm not in civvy street any more, I'm not used to taking orders like this.

On the sands, the troops give us a great big cheer. There are a couple of navy P.O.'s walking up and down near the waters edge, they have revolvers in their hands. I found out later on that they were there to shoot anyone who broke the ranks, but no one did at any time while I was working the beaches. We gave the okay to the P.O. to start the men to come aboard. They had to wade the 250 yards out to us – even then the water still only came up to their waists; although in some cases if a man was very short or stepped into a pothole, he'd get wet all over. Some swam out to us, but the ladders were floating out flat from the sides of the boat, like I thought they would. They had to position a man either side of them to keep them stable. I reached over the safety chains and helped the first man aboard. 'Thanks mate.' He said. 'We've been waiting three days and nights for you – and where's the air force we've been

123

hearing so much about!' I said, 'They're about somewhere mate – and doing a good job according to the wireless!' I told him to go below and make himself as comfortable as possible, then carried on helping others aboard. One of them said 'Aren't you taking us to Blighty?' I said, 'No mate, we're only a ferry boat.'

Some of the others coming aboard, were using the rubbing bands on the outside of the hull as a ladder. Some made it okay – some fell back into the sea. These rubbing bands were about two feet apart and not thick enough to get a proper toe-hold. To climb aboard with a full pack and rifle called for a lot of strength. After a while I started to throw the rifles into the sea. They didn't like that, and a lot of swearing and shouting started. I said '**** the rifles! Lets have you blokes on board – and quick!' Some took the bolts out and put them in their pockets, others threw the lot away. I was to learn later what a serious thing it was to leave a rifle unguarded – never mind throwing it away!

By now we had over two hundred men aboard. I said to Harry 'You had better go astern about forty feet, Harry boy, or we won't get off the bottom.' After that we got about another two hundred and fifty aboard, and we were well and truly loaded. I shouted out to the P.O. 'That's the lot mate – be back later for some more.' We could see the men on the shore were upset as we drew away. I expect they thought their turn would never come.

On the way out to our destroyer, we had to dodge lots of little boats – all loaded and going out to the destroyers, or empty on their journeys back to the beaches. It took about fifteen minutes to get to our ship. On the way, I went down to the saloon to see how things were. Men were everywhere – in the basket chairs, on the tables, lying on the floors – just everywhere! They asked all sorts of questions, including 'Where are the R.A.F.' and 'Where are we going?' Some of them started to give me packets of cigarettes – twenty, forty, sixty at a time. They had loads of them, and bottles of scent. I put them all in a cupboard and locked it up. By that time we were close to the destroyer – we waited our turn to go alongside her – she already looked overloaded, there were troops everywhere.

On another trip later on, I believe this was on the Thursday, I remember seeing a small barge at anchor, a Thames barge of about forty tons – what we call a punt in the trade. I said I'm going to ask the lieutenant if we can run alongside that barge and take the two iron ladders out of her. The lieutenant said it was okay – 'All for the good of the job!' I told Harry to go alongside her. Harry shapes to go alongside the barge, and then changes his mind and goes head on to her. A big wave came and lifted us up and slung us head first at the barge and *Tigris I* didn't like that. There was a big crunching sound – half her stem had broken off showing the pap. She is half rotten. About three planks each side of the stem above the water line have opened up. After a few choice words with Harry, I said to Warren 'Oh well, let's get on with it, give me some rags, grease, hammer and nails.' I then asked one of the naval ratings if he would get us some tea and some grub whilst we did the repair work and got the ladders out of the barge. He soon came back with some strong tea and a meal of corned beef – the first food since morning and it was nearly dark now!

With the repairs finished as best as we could and after checking the engine, we set off for the beach. On the way there Warren told me that we were leaking a bit.

We loaded up again with troops – we did four runs that night, all similar to the first run, but to different ships.

At seven o'clock on Friday morning, the navy patrol boat came up to us with new orders. We were told to run further along the beach and pick up French troops only.

'What about our blokes – that's what we're here for isn't it?' We were told to get on with it – 'Churchill's orders.' We had nothing against the French, only we thought we should clear the beaches of our own men first. I thought, if ever I meet Mr. Churchill, I'll tell him what I was thinking at the time!

We soon got to our new hunting ground – there were more wrecks than ever there. Ships were sunk everywhere, fuel oil as thick as could be and wreckage all over the place. What with this and our new orders it took the heart out of us; but we were tired, and hadn't had a proper nights sleep since Sunday.

We started to load up with French troops – what a sight they looked – dirty, unshaven and obviously very tired and very hungry. Some were crying as they came aboard, they were leaving their own country of course, and loved ones! They looked as though they must have been on the beach for over a week. I was leaning over the stem over the safety chain that went round the boat, helping to pull one of the men up on board. I had somehow got my foot under the flange; he trod on this, squashing my foot – did I shout! The screw had gone through the toe cap of my shoe between my big toe and the one next to it. I showed the Frenchman this and told him what he'd done; but he didn't understand English – just shrugged his shoulders, clapped me on the back and walked on. It had broken the skin between my toes and was very sore.

After we had loaded and got underway, I went down to the cabin and got an armful of fags and gave them to the troops. They were very grateful – I don't think they'd had a smoke for a long, long while. In the meantime the raids by the German aeroplanes continued; we had had a few near misses from both bombs and machine gun bullets. I found myself hiding behind the wheelhouse which was made of three-ply – I don't know what protection I would have got from that!

The ship we were taking the Frenchmen to was now closer inshore, and we were quick to unload and make for the shore again. The sea was still a flat calm, the sky as blue as anything – not a cloud to be seen. Another raid, and we see three of our spitfires chasing five Gerry planes. The AA guns were firing up into the blue sky, and we could see the shells burst and black smoke suddenly appearing, distinctly and unevenly. One German plane got hit and we saw the pilot coming down in his parachute, which was full of holes – he came down out of sight. Then another Gerry plane got shot down, and a couple of minutes or so later, our three planes fly overhead, wagging their wings in victory, and then disappearing, and all of a sudden the sky is clear and blue again – not an aeroplane in sight. The noise from the guns had been loud and long, but now, apart from the throbbing of our engine, all was quiet again. We had been drenched several times from near misses, and the old *Tigris I* was leaking very badly by now. The fly-wheel was going around in the water now, and the pump was going full out.

On the run back to the shore, two of us had to bale out the whole time – we used a couple of old buckets. We noticed an old London tug high and dry on the beach where the tide had left her – she had

had part of her stern blown away; we couldn't see anybody on the decks.

We were all very tired, our eyes red, we could hardly keep them open. We loaded more troops; unloaded these and then went back again; this time we put our boat's head on the sandy bottom and waited for the P.O. to send out more troops.

We decided to have a look around the boat to see what she was like, and didn't like what we saw – she is in a sad and sorry state, and we noticed that some of the windows were blown in, with glass all over the place. We cleaned this up as best as possible, then returned on deck. We noticed that the boat was rolling from side to side, because the fore part of her was on the bottom. The safety chains were off midships so that the troops could get aboard easier. Harry was lurching to and fro with the motion of the boat, his hands in his pockets – all of a sudden she gave a big roll, Harry walked backwards, and was overboard – flat on his back. We all laughed; then pulled him back on board – spitting and spluttering and cursing us for laughing at him. 'Serves you right mate!' I said. 'I've told you before about having your hands in your pockets, but never mind – at least you've had your feet on French soil, which is more than we've done!'

After a couple more runs we loaded up a Tilbury Mud Hopper, but things were getting very bad for *Tigris I* by now. We, the crew, were exhausted and very hungry, plenty of tea to drink but no food. Harry, Warren and I had a bit of a talk – we didn't think *Tigris I* would keep afloat much longer. We told the lieutenant this, but he just said 'Carry on doing the best you can.'

By early Saturday morning we felt like dropping – no wash or shave since last Saturday, and hardly any sleep. My face was itching, my feet all swollen and my body sore all over – I was not alone! We had lost both our iron ladders, but still managed to load up one more time. I had given all the cigarettes away, except for six packets – one each for us. I went to speak to the lieutenant again and said 'we can't hold out any longer!' He agreed. A patrol boat soon came over to us and we were told to abandon ship and break up the engine so that it was no use to Jerry. Warren got the order to break the engine up – he had tears in his eyes – 'What will the old man say?' He protested. 'He'll have to buy a brand new engine this winter!'

127

Harry and Warren weren't long in packing a small suitcase each; I only had what I stood up in. The three ratings, Harry, Warren and me all get aboard the hopper. We apologised to the skipper for keeping him waiting. He said 'Right me lads – we're away.' He gave a double ring on the telegraph and was full steam ahead for Ramsgate."

At Ramsgate, a naval officer said to them, "I hear you chaps have done a very good job," – he heartily congratulated them. Bill noticed that Ramsgate Harbour was packed tight with all sorts of craft – tugs off the Thames, barge towing tugs, lighters, sailing barges, pleasure boats. he had never seen anything like it before.

Also in Bill Clark's account, is the story of their journey back to Kingston – they were still officially in the navy; but that is another story and already part of the basis of a book being written by Steve Hastings, a relative of the publican of Gloucester Arms at Kingston and owner of *Tigris I*. There is a little more about this in the epilogue

Chapter Eight

The Ladies Take a Part – Trains Galore

J im Denne, was in 507 Company R.A.S.C. 44th Territorial Division. They had been dropping off ammunition to various other companies – the last drop being made just near to Cassel before they had decided to break up and head for the coast in small groups. Jim, with three or four of his mates took quite some time making their way to the beaches, eventually arriving at Dunkirk after being moved on from La Panne. They spent some time on the beaches before getting onto a small boat that took them out to a larger foreign ship – possibly a Swedish coalboat. They had had quite a job getting from the small boat to the larger one; they were still carrying their rifles and bandoleers of ammunition. On the way back over the channel they had spent some of their time banging away at sea mines – ones well in the distance of course!

They made it to just outside Dover, but for some reason weren't allowed entry into the harbour; probably because of some mix up because it was a foreign vessel. (There is another piece, later in the book, about a foreign vessel, loaded with British troops, not being allowed into Dover – but having to return to another place in France.) They finished their journey tying up to Margate Pier. From there, after being given refreshments from an A.F.S. canteen, they boarded a train which quite soon stopped at Faversham. By this time Jim knew the immediate route they must be taking. Whilst they were being given some hot food at Faversham from the R.A.F. field kitchens there, Jim spoke to one of the station staff, telling him that his father, Walter Denne, was station inspector at Gillingham railway station, a little further up the line. He asked him if he could get a message up the line to him telling him that his son was on this

129

particular train. A little later, before they left Faversham, the station employee told Jim that his father had just gone off duty after working forty eight hours non stop – seeing the evacuation trains going through. However, Mr. Hunt, the station master at Gillingham had immediately sent the only taxi that operated from Gillingham Station in those days, to his home to collect him.

The outcome was that Jim's father, mother and brother-in-law made it to Gillingham station, where the train came through very, very slowly, allowing Walter Denne to get on and Jim to briefly say 'Hello and goodbye' to his mother and brother-in-law. During the few minutes it took to get from Gillingham to Chatham, Jim told his father as much as he could of what had been going on. Walter gave his son some money and got off the train at Chatham, having completed one of the most meaningful train journeys of his life!

Jim and his mates finished up at the military headquarters at Shrivenham, where they were de-loused, bathed and re-kitted.

This was just one incident that involved the co-operation of the railways at that time, but they played a far larger role in the operation than just this one very human incident.

The staff of Southern Railways were now working furiously to get train after train to the southern ports, to take the troops on their journeys to various parts of the country. But before these battered, weary, dishevelled and exhausted soldiers got onto the trains, the Women's Voluntary Service, The Church Army, Salvation Army, Red Cross and other dedicated people also came to do what they could for them. This included handing out much needed refreshments, giving minor first aid where necessary, providing clothing where urgently needed and doing all sorts of other things to make them just that bit more comfortable. It wasn't only at the main stations, that this help was forthcoming, but also on a lot of the little stations on their routes.

In 'Women in Green,' a book about the W.V.S. Charles Graves writes:

'At first it seemed as if nobody realised the implication of Dunkirk, and the first call on the W.V.S. was for darning needles. Never the less, the endurance and selfless devotion to duty of the W.V.S. reached new heights during this period. The chairman, Lady Reading, had been talking to the Mayor of a coastal town before the outbreak of war, urging him to give his support to the W.V.S. He had said. "The W.V.S. – They'll never stick to it when the time comes – I'll bet you £20 they won't stick it!"

Lady Reading was not a betting woman, but on this occasion she accepted the bet. On her next visit to the town, the Mayor handed over £20 – "I owe it to you," he said, "as the troops returned from Dunkirk in every kind of boat, we showed them into cinemas, churches and halls. As they came in through the doors, many of them fell asleep straight away. You should have seen your women rolling them into lines, removing their equipment, their boots and socks, washing their feet as they lay there; and then taking their socks away to wash them, returning them later. I went round and watched them, and I thought how much the men's feet had bled; but then I looked again and saw that it was not stale brown blood, but fresh red blood that came from the women's hands."

Centre organisers in ports and important railway stations were asked to organise canteens, which opened at short notice and functioned as long as they were needed. The usual stores of the station buffets had to be supplemented with quantities of tea, coffee, milk, bread, sugar and many other foodstuffs, such as cakes, biscuits, sausage rolls and meat pies. As night came, the W.V.S. workers tried to sleep when they could, on hard chairs and floors.

With boats arriving all the time, there was a never ending stream of men passing through the canteens; they continuously answered greetings with a nod or a dazed smile, but they drank the mugs of tea that were thrust into their hands, and then headed for the waiting trains and fell asleep. Great jugs of tea and coffee were carried down to the boats to serve the crews or the wounded men, waiting to be taken away on stretchers.'

In the meantime the trains were running efficiently and smoothly – hundreds of them, with Dover getting the lions share, but stations such as Sheerness, Ramsgate, Margate, Folkestone, Newhaven – even as far west as Southampton, all getting their quota of trains.

For a service that was so often criticised, some people wondered how this remarkable efficiency came to be – who was behind the organisation?

131

The answer was that big occasions such as Rugby Internationals, Cup Finals, The Derby and The Grand National were treated differently – on those occasions the officials knew what they were organising for; but for the troops coming back from Dunkirk there was nothing to go on and a different plan was needed. Improvisation and word of mouth became the order of the day, and if ever the telephone proved its worth, it did so now. The superintendent of operations, Mr. Wheeler, instantly picked his best men and sent them to the scene of action with full powers. Priority for staff, for rolling stock and for telephones was given to them, and they did the rest. "If only," exclaimed a general, "the army could operate with as few written instructions as The Southern Railway does!"

With hundreds of trains becoming available, it was thought that chaos was bound to be the outcome, but everything went smoothly. The procedure that took place, was as follows:

'As soon as the word 'Dynamo' was received, the divisional superintendent at Orpington held a meeting of his assistants, and sub-control offices were set up there and also at Dover Marine, Tonbridge, Ashford, Faversham, Chatham and Dartford. Inspectors were placed at the two stations at Dover, and then the stations at Folkestone, Ramsgate, Margate, Ashford, Headcorn, Paddock wood and Faversham – all stations mentioned here are in Kent. On other parts of the line there were sub-controls at Haywards Heath, Chichester and Shalford. The were two liaison officers appointed who were in constant touch with the military authorities at Dover Marine – one by day and the other by night. Empty trains were held at Queenborough on the Isle of Sheppey, Faversham, Margate and Ramsgate, and the fear of not having enough of these empty trains, and the problem of handling them, were two ever present anxieties, especially at Dover where the numbers of men were sometimes overwhelming. Yet in the end, empty trains from other railway systems came so thick and fast, that at one time four of them were held at Willesden, since they could not be accepted at the ports.

At all the stations, members of the public were quick to join in and help in any way that they could. Some of these had heard about what was going on by 'word of mouth.' Others, like Winifred Thorne, had, as she put it – "Simply come upon this amazing scene going on right in

132

front of my eyes!" Winifred told me, "I got a train at Gillingham to go and see my husband, who was stationed at Canterbury, and probably soon to go overseas. When we got to Faversham we had to pull into a siding so as to give another train priority of passage. This train was full of troops. I could see them quite clearly as they pulled in right beside the train I was on, on the adjoining platform. They were dishevelled, dirty and obviously very hungry – it was like a scene I had seen pictures of, of World War I. My heart went out to them. The people on the station, the W.V.S. and ordinary people like myself, were giving out refreshments, so I thought that I must do something as well. I got the pork pie, sweets, biscuits and cakes I'd got specially to give to my husband, and handed it all to the troops, they were so grateful, one of them even kissed me – I'll never forget it! I remember some of them asked me what the news was – they didn't know anything at all about what was going on, and asked me if I had a newspaper. I hadn't, but I remembered that a man in my carriage had got quite a bundle of them, so I went back to the carriage to ask him if he could spare one or two of them. He wasn't in his seat, so thinking that he'd just gone and left them, I picked up the whole bundle, walked back over to the troops and handed them over. A little later, when our train continued on its journey, the man came back and loudly asked what had happened to his newspapers. I kept quiet; I could feel that I'd gone red in the face – all in a good cause though!"

Later, Winifred had to explain to her husband why she hadn't bought him all the things she promised she would; this explanation was met with a few moments of stony silence – then laughter, as her husband told her that if he'd been in the same position, he would have done exactly the same thing!

Dot Weedon, who now lives at Chatham, told me – "I was in the A.R.P. (Air Raid Precaution) at the time of Dunkirk, and working at Shorts at Rochester, who made the Sunderland Flying Boats. I was a secretary. One day there was a call to the factory asking for members to report to Chatham station, to help to feed all the troops on the trains going through. When I got there I saw that there were people from all walks of life – all eager to help, all keen to do what they could. I remember seeing one man cutting up loaves of bread, he got

133

about six slices from each large loaf – they were like giant doorsteps, but much appreciated.".

Dot told me, 'The manager of the Co-op at Chatham had heard about what was going on, and with help from his staff, took all the 'immediately eatable' food, such as sausage rolls, pies, cheese, bread and all sorts of other things, to the station for the people working there to dole out – "To hell with what my bosses will say!" He said, and with that as a parting shot, he, with his staff trailing behind him, hurried off to fetch some more.'

At Paddock Wood station, Patricia King had arrived to start the journey to her fiancé's parents home at Edenbridge; he was due home on leave there later that day. She had spent months making him a multi-coloured pullover from bits and pieces of wool she had unravelled, and had only just finished making it. She noticed that there were lots of people sitting around tables on the station platform making sandwiches; all of a sudden a train came in – it was packed with troops, most of them looking dirty and scruffy, not like soldiers usually do. Although they seemed quite cheerful, she could tell that they'd been going through some sort of hell. One of them didn't appear to have a coat, so, on the spur of the moment, she handed him the pullover. Patricia told me "I've always been glad I did this. In later years when my husband and I talked about it we always had a good laugh, because, although he didn't say so at the time, he was dreading having to wear it and was more than pleased that I'd given it away."

At Headcorn, where there was only a staff of a station master and two porters, they fed 145,000 troops. The R.A.S.C. provided the food and there were forty soldiers to hand it out, but these forty were helped by fifty or so lady volunteers from the neighbourhood. For nine days and nights they worked in shifts of eight hours each; but eight hours were not enough to satisfy their enthusiasm, and one of them stayed on continuously for twenty four hours. Their Headquarters were in a large barn in a nearby field. This was where the food was made ready and then carried across some fields – then across the railway line, and then onto the 'up' platform. Sandwiches were just one item in a reasonably extensive bill of fare. There were also hard boiled eggs, sausage rolls, meat pies, jellied veal, oranges and apples.

134

As far as tea and coffee was concerned, one of the helpers said – "the whole of Kent could hardly have produced enough cups for the men to drink from, and the refreshing liquids went into the trains in tin cans. When time was up for each batch, the R.A.S.C. on the platform, shouted out to the troops in the train – 'sling them out' – and a shower of tin cans clattered onto the platform – and these would be quickly collected by the amateur and professional staff on the station, washed up and ready for the next train."

When the troop movements had begun, Phyllis Knott and some other members of the W.V.S. at Folkestone, were called out in the night to make sandwiches and prepare other refreshments. In the early morning they were told to make haste to Westenhanger station, just by Folkestone Racecourse. She remembers arriving there on that first day to be greeted by the dawn chorus. "It was just beautiful – and everything else was so quiet, but then the first of the trains arrived, and very quickly everything changed. There was one every quarter of an hour, and you should have seen the troops; they were wet, bedraggled – some with hardly any clothing, and they were all starving hungry. Amazingly, they were mainly all quite cheerful, but I suppose that that was because they were all so glad to be back home. Some of them gave us postcards to send for them – they'd quickly scribbled on them on the journey from Folkestone Harbour, to say that they were okay. It was an experience I shall never forget."

At Margate, things were also all of a bustle early in the morning of the 27th May. Mick Twyman, a local Historian has given me the following account – 'the local police and emergency services were briefed to be on the highest alert as "something had gone wrong over the other side." Many of the people who were involved at that time said that they had no idea of the events that were about to unfold. The ridiculous security decision not to tell them about the B.E.F. in France, meant that they thought that they were probably getting ready for the invasion, which had been a very real threat for some time. To make matters worse, and increase their fears, the Margatonians were dismayed to see the army pulling out of their defence positions around the town to proceed to a new defence line further inland.

The jetty, scene of so many happy outings and events over the years, was mined with demolition charges to deny its use to the

Germans if they arrived, and two sappers stayed behind to blow the charges if required. In the afternoon of the 27th May, personnel of the Royal Navy arrived and took over control of the harbour and jetty, making their headquarters in the Droit House, nearby. There was still no hint of what was going on or what was going to occur over the next few days, and Margate was ill equipped to deal with any kind of emergency anyway. There were no emergency stores of food, blankets or clothing in the town.

Dorothy Parker has vivid memories of that time. Along with the late Nora Doughty, she had been a founder member of the Margate Ambulance Corps when it was formed in the mid 1930's. She recalls how, on May 28th, she and her colleagues were told to "get down to the jetty." When they asked why, no explamation was forthcoming – just a repeat of the blunt order. When they arrived there, the reason quickly became apparent, when, in the afternoon sunshine, vessels crowded with khaki clad cargoes of men from the B.E.F. started to arrive at this famous old jetty. They were daytrippers of a different kind, but just as pleased to see Margate as their peacetime counterparts had been. One cockney soldier was heard to say – "I've enjoyed many happy outings to Margate – but this is the best of them all."

The first vessel to arrive was the *Sandown* which brought 201 men; this was followed by the *Gracie Fields* which brought a further 281. During the following week, over 100 vessels brought to the safety of Margate 46,772 men, which was one seventh of the total numbers evacuated from France.

The emergency services and towns folk all worked ceaselessly to care for the wounded, and there were many of those landed at Margate. They saw to the needs of the exhausted troops, many of whom had lost clothing during their ordeal. The town and the surrounding area were scoured for food and drink to supply the needs of the men, and the townsfolk gladly gave from the meagre stocks in their larders. Appeals for clothing and blankets met with an overwhelming response, with over 2,000 shirts, hundreds of coats and blankets, and plenty of pairs of trousers, even underwear, appearing from the half empty town. The great problem though, during those first few days, was finding footwear – lots of boots had been left in France, but once again the town turned up trumps, with hundreds of

136

pairs being found. Eventually, the army got its act together and supplies of boots began to appear from the quartermasters store at Dover Garrison – some uniforms as well.

Parties of volunteers from the town ranged all over East Kent to secure what supplies could be found – those in Margate soon having been exhausted. The job of feeding the troops went on unabated, and it was estimated that 100,000 cups of tea were served to the troops as they passed through the town on their way to the trains that whisked them away, and they all got something to eat!

East Kent buses were laid on to ferry the troops to the railway station, but first they faced a long tramp down the jetty to the shore. Obviously, there was no time to be lost in getting some of the more severely wounded to the hospitals, and the brave decision was taken to drive the ambulance of the Margate Ambulance Corps up the jetty, in order to speed their treatment up. The jetty had a deck of two inch planks, and its a wonder that the ambulance didn't drop through it into the sea. Some of those present at the time said that the jetty was creaking and groaning as the ambulance went on its way, but it stayed in tact – another small miracle of Dunkirk!

Thousands of stretcher cases were treated at first aid stations set up at Dreamland and The Winter Gardens, while The Royal Sea Bathing Hospital dealt with 500 and Margate Hospital 230 of the more seriously wounded. Many of the cases dealt with at the hospitals were spinal injuries, caused by compression when vessels were on were hit by bombs and blown out from under their feet.

Finally, every effort was made to ensure that all the troops were given either a postcard or a telegram form to notify their families that they were safely back home.

At home, in Brighton, father 'glued' himself to the radio, and made a point of talking to Bruce Belfrage every day before he went off to read some of those days bulletins at the BBC. More news was coming through by now, but father knew that what was being reported was nowhere near the full picture – the real situation. Mother had resigned herself that she wouldn't hear any more about uncle Jimmy until they'd got the B.E.F. safely back home. She now made a point of going to St. Marks church each evening, and offering a few silent prayers for him and anyone else caught up in this bitter conflict.

137

One other person, amongst the thousands who were probably all offering up their own silent prayers for loved ones who were involved, but hadn't been heard from for some time, was Edith Wiggins. She had married her husband Ernie in 1938 – their daughter, Doreen had been born prematurely in April, 1939. They lived in High Wycombe, and Ernie had joined the Supplementary Reserve of the R.A.S.C. in October 1938. After this he had carried on in his job as a bus driver – that is, until the police sought him out, to tell him that he had to join up. What happened was this. On the last day of August 1939 he had stopped for a cup of tea whilst taking a break from taking his bus out; he was standing talking to his conductor when the police car pulled up close to them. "Is your name Wiggins?" One of the policemen asked him.

"Yes," Ernie replied.

"Do you know you've been called up?"

"No," Ernie replied. "Who called me up then?"

"It's been on the radio and in the newspapers."

"I don't listen to the radio much – and I don't read the newspapers either;" Ernie said, "so what do I do now?"

They said, "Jump in the car and we'll take you where you have to go!"

"What about the bus, and also my motor-bike?" Ernie asked.

"You can leave the bus where it is, but we'll take you to your motor-bike – after that report directly to your unit – it's as important as that!" So Ernie was taken to collect his motor-bike; he then drove home, kissed his wife and daughter goodbye, and went to join his unit.

On September 8th 1939, as a member of the Vehicle Replacement Depot of the R.A.S.C. he left Southampton for Cherbourg. He and his unit then spent until the end of September waiting for their vehicles to turn up at the car racing track at Le Mans, which they were using as a collection depot. After this, they moved off in convoy to a village called Flascelles near Amiens; Ernie's section though, was put just nearby at a place called Talmas.

Their lorries and Triumph motor cycles were all practically brand new – they felt proud of them, and looked after them accordingly. Their clothing was a different story though; they were dressed in

1914 uniforms, with puttees, button down tunic fronts and thick webbing – Ernie's uniform had 1917 printed on the pockets.

While they were at Talmas, they noticed German spotter planes taking an interest in them. They soon learnt that the Germans had reached St. Quentin, just over twenty miles away, and within hours they moved off in convoys towards Ypres. After a while, they stopped at an old deserted chateau where the cook got a hot meal ready for them. While they were there, some of the men brought in a German soldier they had captured. On being asked, in halting German, who he was – he had answered in perfect English that he was a sergeant in the German army, and had spent some time at Oxford University! He didn't volunteer any more information and was soon turned over to whoever was looking after German P.O.W.'s – the date was May 12th.

Before long Stuka attacks started, and after a skirmish with the enemy, when they soon realised that they were no match for the German machine guns and artillery, they were told to pull back. They eventually went through Poperinghe, where there was another Stuka attack. "Everything was chaos," Ernie told me, "you could smell the burning flesh – it was a nightmare!"

They spent seven days and nights retreating to the coast just staying for a few hours here and there, and during all this time they had been losing men and vehicles. By the time they got to Hazebrouck, just past Armentieres on the main road to Dunkirk, they only had about twelve lorries left and a greatly diminished amount of men. It was here that they had to get off the main roads, which were packed with refugees and the main target areas of the Luftwaffe. Eventually they got to Cassel, using the quieter roads now for most of the time. There were plenty of refugees here as well, but not as many as on the main roads, where they were on the move with horses, cows, chickens, dogs and carts filled with furniture and mattresses – just about everything they possessed, it was a tragic sight.

When they got to Burges, not far from Dunkirk, there were only about twenty of them left; they had to immobolise the few vehicles they had left – it was heartbreaking! They were told not to go into the town of Dunkirk but make for the sand dunes about half a mile from the mole. They had had nothing to eat for forty eight hours

139

when they got there, and were all starving. After spending a while watching the comings and goings to and from the mole, without seeming to get much closer to it, they decided not to go on to it at that time – it was badly damaged and under constant attack by the enemy in any case. They decided to go back into Dunkirk to look for food. They foraged about for a while, but although they found some water – there wasn't any food.

Eventually they decided to return to the dunes, and spent several more hellish days there. The only food they found were some tins of peas in a damaged lorry. They spent three days queuing in the water, where once again there was chaos, with some of the boats being swamped by too many trying to board them. On the third day of queuing in the water they managed to get on to one of the boats, and were taken to a converted minesweeper, which took them to Folkestone.

Ernie remembers the Church Army and W.V.S. giving them tea, sandwiches and cakes. They got more of these refreshments when the train stopped at various stations on their way to a camp somewhere near the Savernake Forest. After spending a few days recuperating and being kitted out afresh, he got a weeks leave and arrived home to a very grateful wife and a baby he had thought he would never see again.

Back at home, now that the beaches were closed to us, mother had started taking my sister Jill and me for walks over the downs to Ovingdean and Rottingdean; this was a replacement exercise for the swimming, paddling, shrimping and prawning, that had filled up so many hours in more peaceful times. One place we used to pass on these circular walks, if we came back on the overcliff walk from Ovingdean Gap, was the Art Decor building of St. Dunstans – for which the foundation stone had been laid as recently as 1937. On one of these walks we had noticed that there were some ambulances arriving with troops in them – casualties of Dunkirk, we were soon to learn. One of these could have been Charles Young. Charles had joined the 63rd Signals Unit of The Royal Artillery, a territorial unit. When the balloon had gone up and the retreat had begun , they were in Belgium not far from Brussels. Later, they saw their first action at Tournais; it was here that Charles was first wounded – a lung wound. He became one of the walking wounded and sometime later found himself on the beach at La Panne. He arrived there with no rifle – not even his pay book, which for some reason had been taken off him at a casualty clearing station – so he had no identity on him.

After nearly three days on the beach, Charles was wounded again and everything went black for him. He didn't remember what had happened – one moment he had been walking along the beach at La Panne, and the next he remembers is being at St. Dunstans at Ovingdean. He had 'lost' several days in the meantime. Arthur remained blind until 1941, when after much caring treatment his sight became fully restored.

Soon after this, St. Dunstans at Ovingdean had to be abandoned to the navy. It was taken over by H.M.S. Vernon, as was nearby Roedean Girls School. A maintenance staff was kept on for a time, and the operating theatre there was kept in use during all the days of Dunkirk and for a while afterwards The patients and other staff at St. Dunstans were evacuated to Church Stretton in Shropshire.

Ernie Leggett of A Company, 2nd Battalion, Royal Norfolk Regiment, was also hospitalised in the Brighton area, after being wounded whilst fighting an epic rearguard action along the river Escaut. On the 21st May he had seen action in which his company sergeant major, George Gristock, won the Victoria Cross, "He was with my company H.Q. – 100 yards to my right." Ernie told me.

Following being wounded, he was picked up by stretcher bearers and taken to a field dressing station, where he was heavily sedated with morphine. After this he got transported by train and ambulances to the beach at Dunkirk. "I remember I could smell the sea – there was also the acrid smell of smoke, fire and burning oil. There was incessant noise from the Stukas as well, with their fiendish and unearthly sounding sirens attached to the wheels of the planes and the fins of the bombs – the terrifying scream of the plane whilst diving, and also pulling out of the dive. Add to this the sound of the Bofors guns and the shells passing overhead from the German artillery and our own navy, and you have a hellish cacophony of sound in a nightmare scenario."

"Whilst on my stretcher in the dunes, I was completely helpless – a fractured lumber spine, shrapnel wounds covering my whole left leg, and gaping wounds where a large piece of shrapnel had passed through my left buttock and out through the groin. I was naked except for a blanket, and swathed in bloody bandages – I was in severe pain. Every now and again I was visited by a medical officer, accompanied by a nursing sister, to be given a further injection of morphine. Time was meaningless, the incessant noise of war was never ending. I thought of my family at home and vividly saw my mother, father, brother and grandfather sitting by the fire. In reality I pictured my small church of St. Peter, Clippesby, as if I was actually there. The Cross Keys, a silver key crossing one of gold, I could see quite clearly. The keys had captivated my undivided attention as a young boy, and became an omen when I realised the Second Infantry Division sign was that of cross keys.

Above the constant noise, I could hear the calling out of the wounded and orders being shouted out, until once again the MO appeared, and that blessed oblivion which morphine can bring, took over – and I fell into an unconscious sleep."

Eventually stretcher bearers lifted Ernie to the mole, and carried him aboard the hospital ship *St. Julian*. "My next awareness was that I was still alive and smelling fresh sea air – no noise, except for the crying of sea gulls." Ernie told me. "There was a Salvation Army nurse there, handing me a cup of tea – she lit a cigarette for me – 'You are back home – this is Newhaven.' She told me."

Ernie was operated on at The Sussex County Hospital in Brighton. This is quite near Sussex Square. I passed by here on my walks to and from school, and I remember seeing men in hospital blue uniforms, who were long term patients there from the services.

Ernie remained there for a year before being discharged – miraculously still able to walk. He says, "I thank God for my life and feel everlasting gratitude for all those who cared and watched over me during my hours of distress."

By now, there were other wounded soldiers lying on the sands at Dunkirk, and more arriving all the time. Also, more boats were appearing on the scene, including a variety of smaller craft which would speed up the ferrying procedure to the larger ships, and there was now the hope that a much larger number of troops than had at first been estimated, might reach the home shores.

Chapter Nine

Tugs – Death of a Destroyer – More Little Ships

There are a lot of 'unsung' heroes amongst many of the little ships, and this includes some of the tugs. I have written quite a bit about the *Sun* tugs later on in the book, but one tug which I have particular reason for mentioning here is the steam tug *Challenge* – also one of this fleet of tugs.

Before the last war, *Challenge* and other tugs owned by the Elliot Steam Tug Co. at Gravesend, were engaged in towing brick barges from Boom, just above Antwerp, to London.

This trade had begun in the mid 1930's, ceasing when war was declared. *Challenge's* career then became, as with all the tugs working on the Thames, more varied and dangerous. Some of their most dramatic moments came in 1940 in Operation Dynamo. It was not just the tugs ability to ferry troops back to Britain that was so valuable, but that they also did highly essential work in helping ships berthing at Dover and Dunkirk, and also rounding up and towing ships lifeboats and lighters.

At midnight on June 1st, after having received orders to proceed as far as possible to Dunkirk and pick up anything that might need assistance, seven tugs, in single line ahead, led by *Challenge*, passed the North Goodwins – a rare sight! *Challenge* assisted berthing at the east mole and also took small craft in tow – vital and valuable work indeed! I have put a special piece in the epilogue about this tug – rather than here – there is also a special reason for this.

On the subject of tugs, and before telling more of the individual stories of the little ships that went to Dunkirk, I would like to add a few words about a destroyer that was sunk and who's survivors were picked up by tugs. The destroyer, which up until the morning of

143

June 1st 1940, had been playing a leading role in what was going on at Dunkirk, was *H.M.S. Keith*.

At one time during the operation, *H.M.S. Keith* had played host to General Gort and his staff. On Saturday June 1st, the weather had cleared from a misty, cloudy start; but with the dispersal of the clouds, the Luftwaffe continued all out attacks on the shipping in the area. Although the destroyer gallantly fought off the first attacks, she soon ran out of anti-aircraft ammunition and was hit by an attack which destroyed the engine room and holed the ship below the waterline.

One of those on board at the time, was stoker John Cranston; he was one of the engine room staff. John had just been relieved from his watch below in the boiler room at 8am, when *Keith* was struck by a bomb which went down the aft funnel and exploded below deck with heavy loss of life. A second bomb exploded on the stern, detonating the depth charges. John, in his narrative of his experiences says – "*Keith* was mortally wounded and sinking, so it was a case of over the side and into the water."

Eventually, the survivors were picked up by two tugs – the *St. Abbs* and the *Vincia*. Once on board, John and the others had to keep under cover as the Germans were still spraying bullets about. When the air attacks petered out, *Vincia*, with John on board, made her way to England – taking 108 survivors from *H.M.S. Keith* back to the safe berth of Margate jetty.

On disembarking from the *Vincia*, John, barefoot and clad in a wet boiler suit, faced the long trudge over the rough surface of the jetty to the shore. Having survived his ship being bombed out from beneath his feet, and coming through sustained machine gunning unscathed, he suffered the fate of being 'scuppered' by his own side, when he trod on a lighted cigarette end, thrown down by one of the boys ahead of him!

After the ministrations of the ladies of the Margate W.V.S. and other volunteers, he was soon onboard a bus which took him off to Chatham Barracks.

John has been back to Margate since – whilst there he visited the lifeboat house, and was lucky enough to speak to a lady in it's souvenir shop who's mother was one of the Margate volunteers who looked after him and the boys at Dreamland, which had been turned into an emergency reception area during the evacuation.

The *St. Abbs*, an Admiralty steam tug, was blown up herself the day after this with survivors being picked up by the tug *Sun XI*. In the final stages of Operation Dynamo the *Vincia* was also lost.

The lifeboat based at Margate during the time of Dunkirk was the *Lord Southborough*. This was one of the lifeboats which, although it had been towed across the channel to save petrol, had kept its own crew for the evacuations – instead of being manned by naval personnel.

I have included two accounts from the crew of the *Lord Southborough*, one is by the engineer E. Jordan and the other one by the coxswain, Edward Parker – by including both accounts I feel that this gives as close an account as possible of one boat's time rescuing troops from the beaches at Dunkirk.

The first, by the engineer, was written shortly after the conclusion of Operation Dynamo:

'At about 11 a.m. on the 30th of May 1940, at the boathouse, I received a phone message from a Royal Naval official from Dover, requesting to speak to the Coxswain.

I immediately found the Coxswain, Edward Parker, and he got in touch with Dover. Mr. Parker was asked if the Margate crew were prepared to man the Margate Life-Boat and proceed to Dunkirk, to assist in the evacuation of The British Expeditionary Force – he replied in the affirmative, and duly informed the crew which included his brother and nephew. He also had a son in the navy who was helping with operations on the mole at Dunkirk.

We were provided with steel helmets, and awaited further instructions. On instruction, the boat launched at about 5.20 p.m. and put off into the Margate roads where we made fast to an Admiralty barge. A quantity of rations and cigarettes were handed to us, and at about 5.40 p.m. we proceeded in tow to Dunkirk, arriving there just before midnight. As we approached, we could smell the fires which were raging in the town and on the docks – the whole sea front was a mass of dense smoke and flame.

The craft which was towing us, unfortunately touched the sand bank, but we succeeded in running an anchor off for the skipper. He then wished us the best of luck and we went inshore, with the engine

145

running dead slow and a small anchor astern. We got in as close as possible and saw masses of troops assembled at the waters edge. We got about eighty on board at first – they were French; we put off and got them aboard a nearby craft and then returned near to the shore. A British officer swam out to us – he came on board and told the Coxswain that he had a large number of his men further along the shore, and guided us to the spot. He instructed his men how to make their way to us – telling them it was their last chance. They soon came swarming through the water to us, up to their armpits, and practically everyone had his rifle slung across his shoulder. Some had removed their boots and trousers; they were assisted aboard. Among them were several who were badly injured, and their mates were holding them shoulder high on improvised litters. We then put off again and got them aboard another craft. We returned repeatedly to the shore for more troops – many of these we transferred to *H.M.S. Icarus*. Whilst alongside, someone on the bridge shouted to us to lay off; we let go and were passing under the destroyers bow when several German aeroplanes arrived on the scene, discharging bombs and machine gunning – pandemonium reigned for a while! However we were fortunate enough to escape any damage or injury, and later on went alongside again. A large pot of stew was passed to us, and although we were busy in the work of rescuing we managed to help ourselves to some of it now and again – fingers before forks!

At about 7 a.m. on 31st May the wind freshened making it impossible to get to the beach again. Some troops had been drowned in their efforts to reach us through the broken water. The Coxswain reported to the destroyer the circumstances and was told to make a search along the shore for anyone who might be on rafts or wreckage. This was done and quite a number more were picked up. One small motor boat R.N. which had been doing good work along the shore was caught in a heavy swell and rolled over and sank. Everywhere around one could see sunken craft and hear the bursting of shells from the German guns. We were told that these were only three miles outside the town. We could see dive bombing and explosions all over the place, and troops frantically trying to dig out all sorts of small craft which had been left high and dry. Cattle were wandering along the waters edge, looking bewildered, and near to us

146

were the charred remains of one of the popular pleasure steamers *Crested Eagle*.

When there seemed to be little more we could do, a naval whaler was seen in precarious condition, we got it alongside and the occupants, all of them R.N. personnel, came aboard, they were members of a beach party, seventeen of them, including two commanders – Comdr. Kerr R.N. and Comdr. Richardson R.N. We then set course for home, leaving off at about 8.30 a.m. and arriving at Margate at 3 p.m."

I have started the second account by Coxswain Edward Parker, from just after he had received his instructions and was about to leave off from Margate:

'The weather was very fine with a light southerly breeze and we left Margate at about 5.30 p.m. The lifeboat was towed by an Admiralty barge to save petrol and make sure we should not lose company, as the commander knew best where to pick the troops up.

We arrived at Dunkirk about midnight when the barge ran aground on the sand, with the lifeboat also bumping, but afloat. I tried to tow the barge afloat, but could not, but at the commanders request I laid out an anchor on a long length of wire – which, on the flowing tide, was a great help to the barge as the wind veered to the North West blowing fresh, making a lee shore. We could by then, out of the darkness, hear someone calling out, so we went as close as we could to them, and when they waded out to us up to their armpits in water, they proved to be French soldiers, these we took on board and transferred them to the barge. The commander then asked us to get some British troops. We again went in and this time found some men of the Border Regiment. By now it was low tide so we loaded up with the troops (how many I could not say) and they said they had got a couple of stretcher cases, could we take them if they carried them off, and we told them, yes. The weight of the troops had put the boat hard on the sand and we had to wait for the tide to flow. During this time, the Luftwaffe were still bombing, and shells were falling from the German coastal batteries

After putting this load on the barge we again returned to shore dropping stern anchor to help us get afloat. We were joined this time by a whaler from a destroyer and we asked them if they would bring

147

off the two stretcher cases, which they did, and we again loaded and returned to the barge with them.

By this time it was getting daylight and we could see the troops east and west of us stretching along the sands as far as we could see. We again went in, getting a very heavy load and returned to the barge, when he told us to take them to a destroyer which was lying some little distance away. This we did and returned for more. The wind by this time had returned to N.W. and was making a nasty surf on the shore. We continued to make further trips to the destroyer, how many times I don't know, but things were getting bad – troops were rushing out to us in all directions and were being drowned close to us and we couldn't get to them. The last time we went into the shore it seemed to me we were doing more harm by drawing the men off the shore as, with their heavy clothing on, the surf was knocking them over and they were unable to get up. The whaler from the destroyer which went into the shore with us on our last trip was swamped, so was the motor pinnace that was working with the whaler; and so it was all along the sands as far as I could see.

Both sides of us there was not a boat left afloat. All this time we were working very near to Nieuport, and as I could not see that I could do any more good I decided to return. We left about 8.30 a.m. on 31st May. On our way towards Dunkirk we fell in with a whaler with seventeen naval ratings in it, they had found the whaler on the sands with no gear in it and full of water. They got the water out and found enough oars on the beach to get it off the shore far enough for us to pick them up, but as the wind freshened, blowing right on shore, they were barely holding their own. They had no rowlocks, but had got the oars lashed to the gunwales, and had been rowing, trying to get to one of the many ships that were in the vicinity , from before daylight. They were the remains of a party of 150 that had been working on the sands for four days. They were taken on board the lifeboat and their boat cast adrift. We brought them to Margate and landed about 3 p.m. For some reason or other the troops told me they were not allowed to go to Dunkirk to embark. Had they been allowed to do so, it could have been done very much quicker and on my return I asked the Naval Officer to make the fact known to the Authorities in charge.

148

I cannot accurately say how many men we were able to get aboard the destroyer and barge, but I do not believe it was less than 500.'

The actual number that the *Lord Southborough* took off, was closer to 600. For his services at Dunkirk, Edward Parker, the coxswain of the *Lord Southborough* was awarded the Distinguished Service Medal for gallantry. There is more about the Margate lifeboat in the epilogue.

The Ramsgate lifeboat, the *Prudential*, had been a gift to the R.N.L.I. from the Prudential Insurance Company. She was another lifeboat to be towed across to save petrol, but which went with her own crew.

The coxswain was Howard Knight – there was a crew of eight. They had been towed over by a Dutch barge. Just before it got completely dark they could make out the flames from burning oil dumps and warehouses at Dunkirk. Reflected from the glow were the shapes of other boats, almost ghostly in appearance – these could have been anything, even German E-Boats preparing to attack them.

The coxswain in his report says. "A little later we saw that some of these were British boats on their way back home, already filled with troops. Aircraft started dropping parachute flares, they could be seen hanging about in the sky like stars or moons, and for a time we could see the other boats much more clearly – all floating targets in what would otherwise have been the cover of a dark night.

The place was a shambles – there were wrecked boats everywhere, and the beaches were just a mass of men. We let the officer in charge here, one of the naval shore party, take the cans of drinking water we had brought with us, and then started to take the men off."

They used a wherry to tow the men from the very shallow water to the lifeboat, and could only take eight at a time doing this, but the trips were short ones and it didn't take too long going to and fro.

In a calm sea the *Prudential* could take 160 aboard. Whilst all this was going on, so was the bombing and shelling. That night they brought off about 800 men and took them to the destroyers or other large vessels. One of these larger vessels was full of troops and ready to make for England, but had developed engine trouble, so two of the crew from the *Prudential* were put aboard her – to help with their knowledge of the currents in case she came to grief on the Goodwin Sands.

After this, with two men short, they carried on ferrying the troops from shore to ships, until by Saturday June 1st they had taken off a further 2,000 men – they then went back to Ramsgate.

The next morning the *Prudential* went out again, this time helping to bring ashore some badly wounded troops from a boat in Ramsgate Harbour. Two nights later she went out again, in answer to flares, and searched until daybreak looking for boats that had broken down in the channel. They found a small motor boat towing a rowing boat – they were hardly moving. Both of these were loaded with French troops – 68 in all. None of them had any knowledge of the sea, but they had managed to start up the engines of the motor boat and nearly make it across. They had had no food or water for twenty two hours, and were taken on board and brought to Margate.

One of the little ships requisitioned by the navy, was *Naiad Errant*, a new prototype of the then popular Swallow Senior Class of pleasure cruisers. She was owned by Wimbledon solicitor, Ralph Nightingale; he was away when the navy came to the yard she was laying in at Sunbury-on-Thames. They managed to find a crew for her made up from members of the Sunbury Fire Brigade, and they took *Naiad Errant* down to Tough's Boatyard at Teddington. After certain adjustments had been made she was taken down to Ramsgate. It was here that she was handed over to Able Seaman Samuel Palmer.

Palmer, had been in the navy for quite some time – he was a 'stripey,' a three badge man who held the Long Service Medal as well as The Good Conduct Medal. He had been drafted from Devonport to Ramsgate, where he had been billeted with some other seamen for the night in The Funfair Ballroom – better known in those days as 'Merrie England.' He had been put in charge of two motor yachts – *Naiad Errant* and *Westerly*, and had been given appropriate crews for these – opting to take *Naiad Errant* himself.

In company with several other craft they proceeded to Dunkirk. During their journey – when they were about three miles from Dunkirk, Palmer noticed a French destroyer – the *Foudroyant* – making her way towards the harbour. When he looked again a short time later, she had disappeared! She had received three direct hits from Stukas, and the French soldiers rescued from her said, "she went down in less than a minute." Fortunately she wasn't laden with

150

troops and the crew were picked up by *Naiad Errant* from among the debris and oil. Some of the crew were singing 'La Marseilles,' Palmer remembered. These were soon transferred to a French tug which was in the vicinity.

After this *Naiad Errant* did a number of shore to ship trips carrying troops. By this time though, only three of the ships Palmer had come across with were still operating together. One of these went aground, and in trying to tow her off, *Naiad Errant* went aground too. After this, Palmer carried on carrying wounded soldiers through the water to a large ship's skiff which was nearby. When the captain of this ship heard of their predicament, he ordered Palmer and his crew aboard – so they swam out to it. Unfortunately this ship got caught by the falling tide. Some soldiers then started working on *Naiad Errant* and managed to get her clear again. Palmer, then 'procured' some petrol from somewhere, to make sure that they had enough fuel to get them back to Ramsgate. At the beginning of their journey the engines failed, so he ordered some of the troops to break up cabin doors and use the pieces as paddles in order to stop the boat from running into the jetty. After quite a long time they managed to get the engines going again and proceeded on their journey. In his report Palmer says, "Just after dawn I struck Dover dead centre, and then followed the coast up to Ramsgate – arriving there I put the soldiers ashore on the pier. There is more about *Naiad Errant* in the epilogue.

The other boat that had been put in Palmer's charge at Ramsgate – the *Westerly* – he never saw again after briefly noticing her when they first arrived at Dunkirk. What had happened was that by 2.30 p.m. on that afternoon she was on fire after breaking down. Fortunately for her crew she had been sighted and then quickly picked up by the crew of *Sundowner*, a yacht owned and skippered by Commander C.H. Lightoller R.N.R. of *Titanic* fame. He had been second officer on the *Titanic* when she sank, and a chief witness at The Inquiry after the disaster. Comdr. Lightoller was an excellent seaman, and in 1939 had been selected to secretly survey the European coast gaining all the information he could – similar in a way to the adventures written by Erskine Childers in his famous book 'The Riddle of the Sands.' I have included the following piece from Comdr. Lightoller's personal account of the evacuation:

151

"My eldest son F. Roger Lightoller and I, with Seascout Gerald Ashcroft, took her out of her winter quarters at Cubits Yard Basin, Chiswick, on the river Thames, on 31st May at 11 a.m. and proceeded according to instructions towards Southend."

The following is from *Sundowner's* log:

'1st June. Southend to Ramsgate. 3.15 a.m. hove up left in company with five others. Proceeded at seven knots to allow others to keep station. Calm and clear. 9.00 a.m. arrived Ramsgate and entered harbour to obtain charts and sailing orders. Instructed to proceed to Dunkirk for further orders. 10.00 a.m. left Ramsgate by route laid down.

"In Ramsgate, I had been given a set of charts and sailing instructions – giving, as I expected, route buoys, channels etc. Half way across we avoided a floating mine by a narrow margin. Having no firearms of any description, not even a tin hat, we had to leave the latter for its destruction by someone better equipped. A few minutes later we had our first introduction to enemy aircraft, three fighters flying high. Before they could become offensive, a British destroyer, *Worcester*, I think, overhauled us and incidentally drove them off.

At 2.25 p.m., we sighted and closed with the twenty five foot motor cruiser *Westerly*, broken down and badly on fire. As the crew of two plus three naval ratings she had picked up in Dunkirk wished to abandon ship – and quickly – I went alongside and took them on board, thereby giving them the additional pleasure of once again facing the 'hell' they had just left. We made the fartherway buoy at 3.00 p.m. and entered Dunkirk roads shortly after seeing the sinking of a French transport with severe loss of life. Steaming through the wreckage and other things we entered the roads.

For sometime past we had been subjected to sporadic bombing and machine-gun fire, but as the *Sundowner* is exceptionally quick on her helm, by waiting until the last moment and then putting the helm over hard – my son at the helm – we easily avoided every attack, though sometimes were near lifted out of the water. It had been my intention to go right on to the beaches where my second son, Second Lieutenant R. Trevor Lightoller, had been evacuated from some forty-eight hours previously – but the survivors from *Westerly*

152

informed me that the troops were all away from there, so I headed up for the Dunkirk piers.

By now dive-bombers seemed to be forever dropping out of the clouds of enemy aircraft overhead. Within half a mile of the pierheads a two funneled transport had overhauled us on a converging course and was just passing us to port when two salvoes were dropped in quick succession right along her port side. For a few moments she was completely hidden in smoke and I certainly thought they had got her, but she reappeared out of the smoke, gaily steaming on and heading for the piers which she entered just ahead of us. The difficulty of taking troops on board from the quay high above us was obvious, so I went alongside a destroyer – *Worcester* again I think, where I think they were already embarking.

I got hold of her captain and told him, with a certain degree of optimism, that I could take a hundred, though the most I had ever had on board was twenty one. He, after consultation with the military commanding officer said, "Go ahead, take all you can." I may say here before leaving Cubits Yard we had worked all night stripping her down of everything movable, mast included, that would tend to lighten her and make for more room. Roger, as previously arranged, packed the troops in down below, and I'll say this – he packed to some purpose. On deck I detailed one naval rating to tally the troops on board. At 50, I called below – 'how are you getting on?' Receiving the cheery reply, 'Oh, plenty of room yet.' At 75 he admitted they were getting just a little bit cramped, all equipment and arms being left on deck, so I told him to let it go at that and pack them on deck – having passed the word for every man to lie down and not to move. By the time we had 50 on deck I could feel her getting distinctly tender so took no more. Actually we had 130 on board including the three of us on *Sundowner* and the five we had taken off *Westerly*.

During the whole embarkation we had quite a lot of attention from enemy planes, but derived an amazing degree of comfort from the bark of the *Worcester's* anti-aircraft gun overhead. Casting off and backing out we again entered the roads where it was continuous and unmitigated hell. The troops were just splendid and by their own initiative detailed look-outs ahead and astern and abeam for

153

inquisitive planes, as my attention was pretty well occupied watching the course and passing word to Roger at the wheel. Any time an aircraft seemed inclined to try its hand on us, one of the look-outs would just call quietly, 'look out for this bloke skipper,' at the same time as pointing. One bomber that had been particularly offensive itself came under the notice of one of our fighters and suddenly plunged vertically, hitting the sea at some 400mph about 50 yards astern. It was a sight never to be forgotten, so were many others for that matter. Incidentally, it was the one and only time that any man on board raised his voice above a conversational tone, but as the big black bomber hit the deck they all raised an echoing cheer.

My youngest son, Pilot Officer H.B. Lightoller, lost on the very day that war broke out in the first raid on Wilhemshaven, flew a Blenheim and had at different times given me a whole lot of useful information about attack, defence and evasive tactics, at which, I learned later, he was particularly good, and I attribute to him a great measure of our success in getting home."

I should like to add to Captain Lightoller's narrative that with 130 men on board, packed like sardines, they were nearly sunk by the weight of troops on board! There is more about the *Sundowner* in the epilogue.

Lieutenant Nat Vaughn Oliver R.N.V.R., my uncle, was put in charge of one of the 'little ships.' Boats were his life, and after the war he would make his home in a house boat moored in the River Adur in Sussex. I can just remember him telling father about various happenings at Dunkirk but nothing remains clear in my mind. I do remember though that the boat he was in charge of had a woman's name – but that's as much as I can remember, and despite various searches I am unfortunately none the wiser.

One particular boat which had a woman's name, but which I am sure he didn't take over was called *Sylvia*. This 45ft. boat built by The Launch and Boat Company in Southampton in 1913 and owned by Mr. A.J. Anstey of B.M.C. Garages at Maidstone, endeared herself forever in the mind of the harbour master at Ramsgate. He never forgot the way the *Sylvia* returned after she had picked up troops from Dunkirk. She had been machine-gunned, set on fire, and on the port side, just above the water line, was a hole which the troops had plugged with their tunics to keep the water out. He had congratulated her skipper on bringing her back to port so badly damaged and full to the 'seams' with soldiers. On talking to the man in charge of her, the harbour master was more than a little surprised when the man said, "I shall quickly do a bit of a job on the part that's holed – and immediately return!" The harbour master begged him to take into consideration the condition of the boat, but the man was more than determined, and said, "I have seen the sea red with blood, arms and legs and other terrible things – it's a sight I shall never forget. The Lord is with us – the sea is calm, and if she goes down I shall go down with her."

The following day, the harbour master Lt./Cmdr. H.J. Maynard heard a lot of shouting and cheering going on – there were ships blowing their hooters and even the troops returning on other vessels joined in the cheering when they saw *Sylvia* arriving back in the harbour at Ramsgate full of troops again. If she had had to go another mile and the sea had been choppy, she wouldn't have made it – she would have sunk. "When she was moored," the harbour master said, "the skipper walked out of what was left of her wheelhouse and I never saw him again." But he did see *Sylvia* again, and I have written about that in the epilogue.

One of the problems facing the troops when they transferred from the little ships to some of the larger vessels, such as the transports and destroyers, was climbing up the rope ladders or just knotted ropes. Many of them were still carrying their rifles and kit, making the task for some of these exhausted men an impossibility.

One of the exhausted men who found this strength sapping task beyond him, was Bob Brooks of the 65th Field Regiment of the Royal Artillery. After seeing action at Oudenarde and other places, they were given the order – "Do as much damage to your guns, wireless sets and transport as you can in five minutes, then make your way to the port of Dunkirk." Bob, and those with him then found themselves faced with a daunting task ahead of them – a 50 Kilometer walk! The date when they started this long hike was May 28th. When they arrived at the beaches, the sight in front of them was even more daunting than the walk had been – queues of men leading from amongst the sand dunes all the way to the waters edge

155

and beyond. After they'd been there for a while they saw that some ships had arrived, and they were told that they could try and swim out to the ships if they wanted to; although they did seem to be some way out.

Bob says, "Several of us decided to do this, but when we got to a ship, some of our lot went to one side and the rest of us to the other. The ones who went to the other side managed to get on board, but on our side there were only ropes and as hard as we tried, some of us simply couldn't manage to climb all the way – so it was back to the beach only to find we had, of course, lost our place in the queue.

Later, some twenty of us swam out to a Dutch skoot – unfortunately she came in too close and grounded on the sands. We stayed on board for several hours waiting for the high tide to free the vessel, but before this could happen we came under heavy fire from the German shore batteries, and were ordered to abandon ship." This meant that Bob and the men with him had once again lost their place in the queue.

It was soon after this that Bob volunteered his services, after he had heard an officer calling for stretcher bearers – promising that he would get those who did volunteer, onto a ship after they had completed the job. The officer was as good as his word and a bit later Bob got aboard a coastal convoy sloop, the *Kingfisher*, and reached Ramsgate on the 31st May.

In one of the letters I received, this one from a gentleman who's family lived at Ramsgate at the time of Dunkirk, he relates the following story, which concerns a Ramsgate based timber merchant.

On hearing about the difficulty men were having climbing the ropes up the sides of ships he decided to try to see if there was some way he could help. He then spent a couple of hours or so calling on the homes of all the men who worked for him, asking them if they would come in for a few hours that night making small wooden ladders for the boats to use. No one refused his request – but they did refuse to be paid!

Experienced crews were still needed to man some of the boats at this time, and Bob Hilton had been searching to be a part of what was going on – up to then without success. He had been commissioned into the army in 1936, but medically discharged. He

156

knew the river well and was well acquainted with small craft such as *Ryegate II*, a 40ft motor yacht with a 10ft beam – ideal for the job on hand. After convincing whoever he had to that he was the man for the job, he and two others, including a man called 'Shaw' and another man who was simply making up the required number to take the boat across – but paid off when they were out of sight of the authorities – started on their eventful journey.

When they arrived at Dunkirk they found that *Ryegate II* couldn't get right to the sands, so they tied up behind a Dutch Schuit (skoot) – the *Horst*, and commandeered a ships lifeboat laying nearby. They then rowed to and fro from the shore to the larger ships laying off shore – one of these being a destroyer. Bob said, "We stopped for a breather and some refreshments aboard this destroyer and all the time there was plenty of activity from the Luftwaffe bombing and machine-gunning and I remember there was a radio playing on board – 'Children's Hour' – it seemed strange to hear this with all the activity going on around us!"

After this they carried on ferrying the troops, sometimes getting swamped and the boat turning over – but quickly put right by the troops eager to be away from all the mayhem as quickly as possible.

At the end they were taken home in a steamer, and *Ryegate II* was towed home. Later on Bob did manage to join up again – this time in the navy – winning the D.S.C. as Lt. Commander R.N.V.R.

In the meantime it was becoming increasingly difficult to continue evacuating the troops from the beaches at La Panne. This meant that the little ships were now being directed to the beaches closer to Dunkirk, and troops arriving at La Panne now found themselves with a long walk across the sands, frequently having to take cover from the increasing activities of the Luftwaffe.

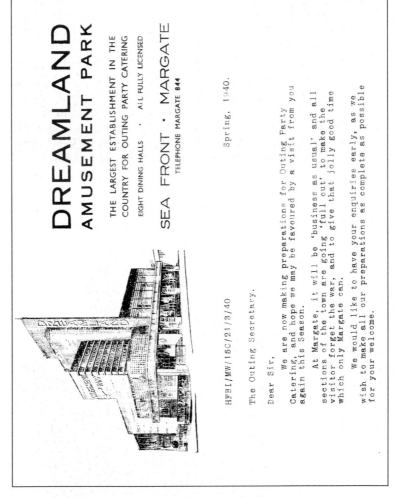

DREAMLAND
AMUSEMENT PARK

THE LARGEST ESTABLISHMENT IN THE
COUNTRY FOR OUTING PARTY CATERING

EIGHT DINING HALLS · ALL FULLY LICENSED

SEA FRONT · MARGATE
TELEPHONE MARGATE 844

Spring, 1940.

HFBI/MW/15C/21/8/40.

The Outing Secretary.

Dear Sir,

We are now making preparations for Outing Party
Catering, and hope we may be favoured by a visit from you
again this Season.

At Margate, it will be 'business as usual' and all
sections of the town are going 'full out' to make the
visitor forget the war, and to give that jolly good time
which only Margate can.

We would like to have your enquiries early, as we
wish to make all our preparations as complete as possible
for your welcome.

"An optimistic outlook at that time – unfortunately history changed such pleasant prospects!"

158

'Call out' – A service launch of "RN Lord Southborough" Margate Lifeboat

A prewar picture of the Ramsgate Lifeboat – Prudential – after a rescue – crew and survivors on board

"Letters home – All shipshape here!"

French soldiers hoping that these letters will get back across the channel

"Back at Dunkirk – Devastation strewn all over the place!"

161

H.M.S. Anthony

Frank Brookshaw on board H.M.S. Anthony

"Sundowner – in more peaceful times"

"Sylvia" (now "Wendy Ken") a recent photograph of her on the River Medway

"Tigris I. – Pre war days on the Thames"

"Naiad Errant" in 1939

164

The tug Challenge on the Thames

The tug – Sun XII
$14\frac{1}{2}$ years old Albert Barnes helped on board during Operation Dynamo

Sun XV – "A very gallant little ship – one of the last to leave Dunkirk."

Going home after a job well done – A tow back up the Thames

Chapter Ten

Long Walks to the Coast and The Beaches of Hell

B y first light on June 1st Operation Dynamo had succeeded in getting a far larger number of troops back to the UK, than had at first been thought to be conceivably possible. It had been thought that the port would have been occupied by the Germans by this time. However, there were still thousands of troops on the beaches, with more troops arriving all the time. Most of those arriving at this time were on foot, but none the less, the huge amount of vehicles that had arrived on and near to the beaches, and which by now had been put out of action and deserted, had given the whole of what had been a pleasant looking stretch of sandy beaches, the new appearance of an ugly and disorganised military dumping ground.

John Mulloy of the R.A.S.C. told me the following:

"I can recall having to abandon our transport in a village some distance from the beaches – this was with the exception of one three ton Bedford lorry – all our personnel had somehow managed to get into this, we were crammed in like sardines; even the tailboard was let out horizontally so men could stand on it, and the cover of the lorry was slashed open to provide some fresh air. There was a large tea chest full of packets of cigarettes in the lorry; after helping ourselves to what we wanted of these, we started chucking packets out to people as we passed them down the roads and lanes – I think they were much appreciated. We finally reached a canal where the lorry was abandoned and I retrieved my kit and rifle. We crossed the canal by walking over a plank, one at a time; a French soldier with a drawn pistol was there to make sure there was no frantic rush – it was the only plank. We eventually passed a house where there was a couple with young children; they were cooking a meal, despite all this going on – they allowed us to draw some water from their pump.

Later, we walked along a road towards the beach and found the sands covered with men – some in queues leading into the sea. I can recall walking along the sands and finding hundreds of abandoned rifles and small kit; each rifle loaded with ten rounds, but each with the bolt missing.

I was amongst a group of men watching as a dive-bomber attacked a navy destroyer – *H.M.S. Grenade*, I believe, it was only about a quarter of a mile out. I actually saw a bomb go down the funnel and explode below deck. The ship gave a great leap out of the water and then settled back again, listing to one side and with smoke and steam coming from it. Suddenly someone in the crowd shouted "Look out – torpedoes." – we looked and saw two silvery, long torpedoes hurtling towards us. We all panicked and tried to run away but the sand was soft and our boots slipped, so we threw ourselves down and waited for the big bang. After a few seconds we heard a loud buzzing noise, like a swarm of angry bees would make, and peering cautiously from under our steel helmets, we saw the two torpedoes spinning about furiously at the waters edge. It was then that the penny dropped, and we realised that whoever had released the torpedoes, had first of all rendered them safe!

During the next day I saw two men who had stripped off their clothing with the intention of swimming out to a destroyer; as they began their swim, a small launch suddenly came into view – it was travelling parallel to the beach. The two men waved the launch down, and although it was not possible to hear what was being said, it was obvious that they were asking for a lift to the destroyer. The person in the launch vigorously waved his arms and shook his head – he was refusing them. By this time the two swimmers had taken a grip on the rear of the launch – one on the right, one on the left. Suddenly the person on the launch opened up the throttle and sped off, with the two swimmers hanging on for dear life – their bodies extended in the sea. The swimmer on the right, quickly lost his grip and disappeared into the sea. The last I saw of the launch was going at full speed in the opposite direction of the destroyer, with the swimmer on the left still desperately hanging on with both hands.

I have no idea of the nationality of the person on the launch, or why he refused the swimmers or what happened to them, but the incident has remained imprinted in my mind.

The following night, after spending another day on the beach, a queue was formed again – it appeared we were going to be lifted off. The hours went past, and then, when the tide began to come in during the early hours, a ships lifeboat appeared – I remember it was just beginning to get light. The boat was crewed by a young sailor who didn't look much more than seventeen years of age, an older seaman was in charge. They shouted to us that they couldn't come in any closer and that we would have to wade out to them. When my turn came I found the sea bitterly cold, and when the water reached my stomach I began to gasp for breath and half decided to turn back as I couldn't swim and was terrified of deep water. However, I kept going until I reached the side of the lifeboat, by which time the water was up to my chest – I was well over six foot tall. The men on the lifeboat hauled me over the side, and when it was filled up a naval launch appeared and towed us to the destroyer, *H.M.S. Codrington* – where we all clambered aboard.

After a short time, and when the ship had got underway; I was standing on the open deck when a sailor came up to me and said, 'Sorry – Captain's orders mate – I've got to have your rifle and ammunition.' I was reluctant about this, but happened to look up to the bridge and saw the captain, with two or three days of stubble on his chin, and not the sort of person to argue with, so I handed over the rifle and bandoleer of ammunition.

On docking at Dover, I was surprised to see lots of rifles being lifted off the ship, and deposited on the quayside. I have never been able to fathom out the captains decision to relieve the troops of these – I always thought a soldier was never parted from his rifle! After this we were ushered onto trains, and I eventually ended up at Winterbourne, an R.E. depot near Salisbury."

When war had first been declared, apart from all the people who suddenly found themselves called up, there were quite a few from other countries who were keen to come and join the action, and who quickly volunteered. One of these was Tom Whelan, who lived in Southern Ireland, a neutral country. He told me the following story:

170

"As a young Southern Irishman, footloose and fancy free, I was anxious to become a soldier, and having seen the poster – 'Join the army and see the world,' I decided that that was the life for me, and took the boat from Rosslare to Liverpool. I then travelled to Warrington, where the South Lancs Regiment had their depot – I enlisted there.

After a medical, it was decided that I was the right material for the Royal Artillery; this suited me very well, having been involved with horses from early childhood – I had visions of becoming a horse gunner and chasing the enemy through the 'Kyber Pass!' Instead I was posted to the R.A. depot at Woolwich, where I did my recruit training as a field gunner. From there I went to Preston Barracks in Brighton, where I joined 107 Battalion, 32nd Field Regiment, R.A.

It wasn't long before we were sent to France and then to the Belgian border, where we spent months digging and preparing defences – which we never used. When the balloon went up, we thought we were off to defeat the Hun, but the boot was on the other foot, and we eventually found ourselves retreating towards Dunkirk. We were on foot, having been ordered to destroy our vehicles and our guns. I remember our officer telling us, 'We have lost the battle but not the war!'

We reached the beach at Bray Dunes, to find a chaotic situation. On the shoreline, there were floating bodies everywhere – mostly sailors; both British and French, washed up from destroyers sunk by Stukas, just a short time earlier. What a sight – beyond description! What a time to arrive at – a holocaust! However, we noticed that troops were being taken off the beaches a bit further along.

Some semblance of order soon turned a chaotic situation into something more orderly, when we came under the direction of armed naval shore parties, and queues were soon formed for the boats. We joined a queue further along, near the east mole. We sat on the sand, making sure we didn't lose our places, and taking pot shots at the Stukas as they came to bomb the mole – we wondered if it would still be there when our turn came.

We were footsore, weary and very hungry, our food and cook had been lost in the bombing – we didn't mind about the cook too much, we'd often threatened to shoot him – but we did miss the occasional hot meal. One of our group, 'Mad Joey,' said '**** this for a game of soldiers,' and dashed across the beaches to the houses on the seafront, quite a few of which were ablaze from the bombing. He disappeared, and a bit later a few of us went to find him, but without success. He eventually returned at dawn next day, looking quite pleased with himself; he had spent the night in a cellar with a group of civilians, who had made him welcome – even giving him food and wine. We could have strangled him – he was always a lucky devil!

We eventually got onto the mole, where moored alongside was *H.M.S. Malcolm.* We had to negotiate a narrow plank to get onto the ship, and I soon found myself in the bowels of the ship drinking a cup of navy cocoa. After this I went to sleep and didn't wake up until we arrived at Dover, where we were given a marvellous welcome. The only black spot was having my rifle taken away from me – I had had this all through the campaign, and it really hurt having it taken from me, I can even remember its number, 72916. After this we boarded a train and ended up at Dorchester.'

One man who used his culinary prowess to the advantage of those who travelled with him on the retreat to Dunkirk was Aubrey King, who had been trained in the Militia as a machine gunner (Vickers 303), and had joined the 1/7 Battalion Middlesex Regiment, stationed at Salamanca Barracks, Aldershot – this is what Aubrey has written:

'I was called up on the 15th July 1939. At that time I was working as chef in the ground floor kitchen at the Cumberland Hotel, Marble Arch, London. The hotel had five kitchens and a huge staff. On arriving on the parade ground we were lined up and called to attention by a Sgt. Major, then port arms for inspection. On inspecting my rifle, he said, 'Dirty rifle King!' I did not recognise him and no more was said, but later that day when speaking to another soldier (they were a territorial battalion) I was told Sgt. Major Knight had been a kitchen staff worker at the Cumberland Hotel – I didn't know him, but he knew me!

At Christmas, I was asked to assist in the kitchen – I did so, and the cook Sgt. Who was too old to go abroad, said he had recommended me for Sergeant cook. Anyhow it never happened and early in January we left for Portsmouth, and overnight went to Cherbourg – I was in Sgt. Major Knight's company. After three days of awful weather we arrived at Houplin, not far from Lille. After a few days A and B Coys decided to join up and have an officers' mess, because they were some distance from HQ. I got the unofficial job as cook – I believe through S.M. Knight.

Early in February, General Montgomery had taken over command of the 3rd Division, part of the 2nd. Corps. He came down to inspect us. Colonel Pringle was C.O. and Major Cunliffe was 'A'.Coy. Commander. General Montgomery said to Col. Pringle, 'You have a fine body of men.' Monty was a very small man – Colonel Pringle, very large; on hearing Monty's words, his chest swelled out! Then, Monty – without any warning, called out – 'GAS!' this was to make sure that we were prepared for anything that might be 'thrown' at us. Unfortunately, except for us Militia men, the rest were territorials and had boards in their gas mask haversacks, and capes rolled around cardboard shell cases – just as they would do on peace time parade, but now they were on active service! The parade was dismissed and we lost our C.O, Adjutant and 'A company' Commander – I'm not sure of anyone else. Colonel Rackham became our C.O. – and then we were really smartened up!

I remained unofficial cook of 'A' and 'B' Coys – our mess was in a beautiful house owned by the family Delcambre, Rue Roger Salengro, with whom I became very friendly. Only the grandmother lived there, her son and family lived in Seclin a couple of miles away.

By the 18th May, we were at a place called Chateau Merode near Ers Kwerps (we were second in line to the battle front on the river Dyle). As we were not getting rations sent up, and were extremely hungry, Sgt. Major Knight decided that the ducks on the moat would make an excellent meal. Ten of these were duly killed and plucked. The Sergeant Major and I explored the chateau, which had been hastily evacuated by the owners, and in the cellars we found wine, smoked hams and bottled vegetables. The S.M. left me there on my own and I prepared lunch (a bit late!) – 'Canard Bourguignonne' a real classic dish! As there was no sign of anybody, I came out of the chateau to find the unit was leaving in a hurry – I didn't have time to return for my gear even, I just jumped on the

173

truck, and we were away! I have often wondered what happened to that beautiful meal.

On arriving at the river Escaut near Tournai, the Battalion H.Q. were in a grand house that belonged to the chief of police. Here, I prepared a pig for us – another special meal, which we managed to eat this time.

From here we made a big move to the last defences. Our H.Q. was at Oostdunkerke and our platoon was on the Nieuport canal near Wulpen, where we had a machine gun in a clump of trees on the left of the road, close to the iron bridge going over the canal – the bridge was blown up. It was early morning on Friday 31st May when we knew the Germans were on the other side of the canal. I was bringing up ammunition to the gun and because of the activity, I was using the muddy ditch which ran alongside the road in line with the gun. We must have been seen by the Germans for I had two mortar shells literally land at my feet. Because of the deep mud they didn't explode, but a third shell hit the gun, putting it out of action.

Later, after several hours more action, including having to drag an injured soldier of the East Lancs on a ground sheet over an exposed area to get him to a first aid post, near our H.Q, we were ordered to man another machine gun on the right hand side of the road – looking up to the blown bridge; the Lancs had been guarding some lock gates near here. As we neared the gun it got hit. The soldier with me was badly injured, but I only had a cut on my right index finger. There was no more action until about ten thirty that night, when we were pulled out and moved down to the coast.

At Oostdunkerke we picked up more of our battalion and then moved on to Sint Idesbald where we were told to rest in the sand dunes while the trucks were destroyed. When the whistle blew, we were to form up lines on the road and march to the beach. I did not hear the whistle and got a bit stressed on my own looking for somebody I knew. As I knew they were marching to the beach I walked down to the shore, turned left and expected to catch up with them. By the time I arrived at the outskirts of La Panne, it was getting light and there were not many troops around. I did not see the 1/7th but I did see one of the naval shore party, with a signal lamp. I asked him what was happening. He answered, 'Since you lot left the canal, the Germans are right behind you, and no boat will pick up at La Panne – your best bet is to make for Dunkirk.'

At La Panne proper, I approached a large group of soldiers – including some of our own; a lance corporal told me that our battalion had marched through the town and that there had been a lot of casualties. He also said it was every man for himself now, so we paired up and started on the 15 kms to Dunkirk. It was a shambles there with all the shelling, bombing and strafing. We got used to this and by watching the dip in the aeroplanes wings, we moved quickly in the opposite direction! Lots of soldiers, French, Belgian and British, were just sheltering in the sand dunes. Ships and boats were being bombed and lots of bodies being washed up on the shore.

A little later we came across a motor bike and tried to start it, but no luck, so we carried on. When we got to the frontier at Bray Dunes there was some sort of defence being organised We did not get involved. Finally, we got to the mole at Dunkirk, where there was a boat alongside – getting to it was like an obstacle race as the mole was full of holes. Finally we got on the boat, which was very crowded – it was called *'Ben My Chree.'* Some bombs were dropped at this time, but missed, and we pulled away. A short distance further out we passed another boat which was sinking – but we didn't stop. The time was 1 p.m. Saturday 1st June. We arrived in Folkestone in a daze, and eventually got on a train which took us to Bridstow in Devon. After that we rejoined our battalion at Corfe Castle in Dorset.

The officers mess cook had been killed at La Panne, and before even getting settled – I was quickly dumped into that job!'

William Boultby, of the 2nd Battalion Northamptonshire Regiment, had fought brief rearguard actions here and there on the retreat to Dunkirk. Armed with rifles and fifty rounds of .303 ammunition each, which they carried in cloth bandoleers, they faced a daunting task against the might of the mechanised German machine guns and other types of more sophisticated weapons than they had – especially as they had been given the order only to fire when fired upon! Most of the food they got they had to scrounge for, but they managed to survive on what could be termed – an oddly assorted diet – carrots from the fields, eggs from hen coops in isolated farming areas and even some chocolate. On their travels towards the coast they had come upon a chocolate factory, and apart from the chocolate they took from there they also helped themselves to a quantity of hazel nuts – nutrition at least!

Later on their journey to the coast, Bill was hit in the hip by shrapnel. A field dressing was put on the wound and he was put on a stretcher and taken by ambulance to Dunkirk Harbour. He spent three days and nights laying on the stretcher, attended to by some military policemen, who brought him sandwiches and some water. After this he doesn't remember much until waking up back in England – his first memory is of being given cakes and tea by the Salvation Army at Paddington Station, before going on to Hospital.

Another member of the B.E.F. who spent several days on the beaches was James Cowley. He had joined the 13th Troop Carrying Company of the R.A.S.C. early in 1940. This was a company of 480 officers and men – the C/O was Major John Houchin. During the first week in May they took delivery of all their transport and made for Southampton, where they boarded the ferry *Antwerpen*. Their destination was Arras, but orders got changed on route and they were ordered to pick up some Grenadier Guards from a set place near to Brussels – the retreat had begun. They were attacked by Stukas and had to dive for cover; most of them survived this, but the refugees that were congesting the roads, took quite a battering. Jim says "I was sick to my stomach as we moved the dead women and children to the side of the road. I tried to move a small girl, but her leg came away – her body stayed put – you have to imagine the horror of this!

We waited at the designated place for about an hour, and then the guards arrived and we took them to a village called Tec.

For the next two weeks, night and day, we transported regiments to different places; we were constantly on the road – one driving whilst the other one tried to get some sleep, but sleep was impossible under these conditions.

On May 23rd, our column took off for St. Omer and Aires. We saw plenty of troops here, including infantry which consisted of men returning from leave and hospital. Some had rifles, some did not, but

176

they were all in it together, and if a man was killed or wounded, his rifle would be passed on. There were a lot of men from the Pioneer Corps amongst these troops.

I remember we were resting for a couple of hours in a forest when a troop of French Colonial Cavalry went through quite close to us, they were mounted and had the robes of Spahis. When we left here I was given a Lewis gun and told to cover the road until all the trucks had left the forest. We were then ordered to a small town called Merville, but the bridge there was closed and there was no entry into the town. We were joined by a troop of French soldiers with 75mm S.P. guns – they were also told that there was no entry."

Jim went on to say that he argued with the sentries that it would be better for everyone if the guns were in the town, and eventually they got permission to enter. They spent a quiet night in this town, which was held by the 5th Battalion Northumberland Fusiliers; they then moved on to 'Proven' to pick up General Gort's H.Q., but they soon found out that they had already gone – two days earlier in fact!

With the retreat now gathering in momentum and the Germans not far away, they were halted and told to select just two of their wagons and destroy the rest. Some of these were only about a month old – it was a heartbreaking job. They were told to make for Calais at first, but because of the situation there, the order was changed and they were told to make for Dunkirk. When they marched onto the sand dunes there, they were attacked by Stukas and they quickly scattered. It was getting dark by this time, so they lost contact with some of their men after the scramble for cover. What remained of their group, made for the beaches at La Panne, where they found some of their company dug in near to a coastguards lookout.

During the next three days they joined various queues leading into the water, only to find that the boat they were queuing for had filled up, and with nothing else coming in they returned, soaking wet, to the sands.

Jim got fed up trying this, so he started to walk along the beaches to Dunkirk. Eventually, when nearly there, an officer told him there was a destroyer about to come into the mole. It took him quite a time to join the queue there – but he made it. He says "About

177

twenty yards along the mole we stopped so the wounded on stretchers could be passed over our heads and onto the destroyer. Quite soon there was a shout – "No more!" I swung my leg over the ships wire rail as it cast off. A very large sailor grabbed me, put me down on the ships deck and told me to go down the companionway. I tried to go down it facing forward, and fell with a clatter onto the deck. A sailor popped out of a doorway and said, "what the hell are you playing at Jim?" I looked up, and there stood Bill Morley, who lived close to where I live. He was the cook, and he soon had me eating a good meal – he gave me forty Ships Woodbines as well. He asked me if I had seen his brother who was with the Sherwood Foresters, but I hadn't. We were having a good natter and drinking tea when a C.P.O. ordered everyone below decks. We were on *H.M.S. Intrepid* and I felt as safe as if I were at home. I remember I went on deck for a brief spell and could see the clock tower on Calais Harbour. As we passed,

I saw that the decks were awash as we swerved and turned to escape shell fire from the German coastal batteries – we went unscathed, and soon arrived in Dover. There are a lot of us who owe our lives to the navy – they were brilliant! Jim was soon on a train which took him to Bulford Camp, Aldershot. After a very long sleep, he went back to normal duties, and the rest of the war.

Another soldier to arrive on the beaches at that time was Joe Lann of 72nd R.A. he had taken part in the counter attack at Arras. Later on, on the retreat, he was in a 30cwt. Truck in company with a seventeen year old gunner, a quartermaster sergeant and the driver; they had been told to make their way to the coast. They had no maps or compass, but on seeing German tanks approaching them they decided to go in exactly the opposite direction! There were refugees everywhere – making the journey extremely difficult. Joe Says, "When an aeroplane strafed us – we stopped the truck and dived into a ditch. The driver was reluctant to go any further, but I threatened to shoot him if he didn't; I believe that if I hadn't done this we wouldn't have made it to the beaches."

In his letter to me, Joe also speaks of peoples reactions at the time of action in war. He remembers seeing one man, a sergeant, who was all mouth and bravado before a battle – he had even offered to fight Joe

178

for some unknown reason, but when the action started, he had to be restrained by four men from running wildly away. Joe remembers thinking when this happened, – "Who can tell how anyone is going to react in the face of enemy action for the first time?"

Joe made it to the beaches where he spent three hungry and nightmarish days and nights. Eventually, after running the gauntlet of enemy fire along the jetty at Dunkirk, he boarded *H.M.S. Winchelsea* which took him to Dover. Sometime later, he arrived at the Regimental Office at Knutsford near Crew, where one of the staff was holding a telegram that he was just about to send – reporting him missing!

With the invasion of the home shores now looking to be inevitable, evacuation of some schools was already taking place around the south eastern coastal towns; some had already gone and there were plenty more to follow. The situation was very tense – especially for parents. Apart from all the newspaper reports on evacuation of schools, my parents had also learnt that there was a growing worry amongst the parents of girls attending St. Mary's Hall School nearby. My sister was at this school and I attended the kindergarten there as well. However, it wouldn't be until later in the month that the school would have to close for the duration – there simply wasn't the money to evacuate to somewhere further away from what looked like becoming a front line area.

Also back at home, with the news from France now coming in all the time, father made a point of buying copies of every newspaper on sale each day at our local kiosk. In the pleasant weather we were having at that time, he would sit out in the top gardens of Sussex Square, carefully reading every word that was printed. There were usually two or three of his friends sitting here with him, so the copies that he provided were well 'thumbed' through. I remember at the breakfast table one day, he read out from The Daily Sketch, a paper he had never bought before, the following:

'One man died and another was seriously injured when sentries fired on a car that did not stop on the main road near Stapleford, Essex.' Commenting on this father said, "I suppose that this is only to be expected now – I dread to say it, but it surely won't be long before we'll be invaded ourselves, and there are probably fifth

179

columnist about everywhere getting prepared for this – especially in the east and south-east!" The same paper also said in another article – 'Surgeons perform operations near the beaches under terrible conditions.' The reporter was told, 'The R.A.M.C. doctors at Dunkirk have drawn 'lots' as to who should remain with the wounded, and three gallant doctors have given up all idea of leaving, unless all the wounded can be rescued!' The article went on with some words about the much criticised 'presence' of the R.A.F. The reporter on The Sketch at that time – J.L. Hodson, said, 'In talking with the officers and men of this returned but unbeaten army, scraps of German military technique emerge. A Brigadier explained to me how, before the bombing, the enemy will send up his fighters to attract our fighters and exhaust their flying endurance in time and petrol, so that when our Hurricanes and Spitfires have had to withdraw, his own bombers can have a clear field.'

One 'lighter' piece of news at this time, came in a telephone call from my father's uncle – W.L. (Lance) Knowles, secretary of Sussex County Cricket Club – he had played as an amateur for both Susssex and Kent. He told father that one officer that they both knew, from those of the B.E.F. that had returned – on arriving in London, had phoned Sir Pelham (Plum) Warner, asking him, "What about a game between a B.E.F. eleven and an M.C.C. team." Sir Pelham had immediately agreed and said that it could even take place as soon as the following week – at Lords!

In the meantime, at the defence perimeter not far from Dunkirk, grim and determined battles were still taking place; but it was only a matter of time, and not much of it, before the Germans would break through completely, making any further escape from the Dunkirk area impossible.

What time did remain, was now of even more critical importance. Stragglers were still arriving on the scene, and the rearguard men, including very large numbers of French troops, were also arriving in the hope of being taken off by what ships there were available – crewed by brave men who dared to venture close to this 'now sinister' place by the sea.

Chapter Eleven

Rearguards – Not Much Time Left

Towards mid-day on June 1st, Captain Tennant, on the beaches near Dunkirk, knew that they hadn't got more much than another day to complete the evacuation. However, things were going quite well at that time and plenty of troops were getting off from the beaches, despite the persistent attacks by the Luftwaffe.

One of the new arrivals on the beach at this time, was Arthur Ayres of 211th Field Park Company, Royal Engineers – attached to the 44th Division. He had been lucky enough to come through an incident packed journey to the beaches, get on a ship for home and then, just when everything seemed to be going well, found himself put back on French soil – this time the enemy being British red tape!

Before explaining how this situation came to be, it is necessary to pick up Arthur's story from earlier on during the retreat. He has written the following account for me:

"We were holding a 'top of a hill' position, not far from the Belgian border. Later that afternoon, which I believe was 30th May, we saw advanced units of the German army moving towards us through a valley. Line upon line of little black dots moved slowly forward through the fields, and as they got nearer we could see their field grey uniforms and bucket shaped helmets.

We had been told to hold this position at all costs and as I glanced at my companions, who lay in a line either side of me, I wondered what was passing through their minds at that moment. This was our first major engagement with the enemy and I wondered what it would feel like to shoot to kill those fellow human beings, who happened to be the enemy – knowing they would be shooting to kill me!

As it turned out, I wasn't to find out at that time as a motor bike roared up – 'Pack up, you chaps,' the rider shouted, 'we're leaving – it's every man for himself now! You are to make for a town on the coast called Dunkirk.' With one more hasty look at the advancing Germans, who were much nearer by this time, I joined the scramble back to the village.

The village was in turmoil; soldiers and civilians were running everywhere, and to our consternation all the company trucks had gone – along with the officers and senior N.C.O's, leaving us to find our own way to Dunkirk.

'Which way to Dunkirk?' I asked a motor cyclist, as he revved up his engine.

He replied – 'Make for that black smudge in the sky, that's Dunkirk!' Several elderly villagers watched our departure, their grim faces showing the anxiety they felt for their future. Their reproachful looks made me feel we had let them down.

The column of people – soldiers and civilians, snaked slowly along the road. They came to a main road which was fast becoming jammed with all kinds of transport heading away from the advancing Germans. Farm wagons chugging along, steam belching from their radiators and loaded with furniture, bedding and household effects. There were also horses with carts similarly loaded, and people with just hand carts – their loads tied down with ropes. The hopeless looks on the peoples faces told it all. I walked beside them heading for that black cloud in the sky, and saw a British stores depot on the side of the road – it was being methodically stripped bare of all its contents. As I passed I was handed a tin of corned beef, a packet of biscuits and a mug of strong naval rum. All of a sudden, a French army officer, mounted on a large cavalry horse, rode by. Suddenly, a British soldier who appeared to have had more than his ration rum, pushed past me and staggered over to the horseman. The horse, frightened, reared up, and the rider raised his whip to the soldier who swore loudly and pulled the officer to the ground. Grabbing at the saddle, the soldier pulled himself up and sat astride the already frightened animal, which bounded forward and galloped off down the road. The French officer by now on his feet, drew his revolver and fired several shots after the disappearing horse and rider. I had to laugh at this unexpected incident, and often wonder if the soldier made it to Dunkirk.

Soon, the light began to fail and darkness set in, but I kept going – guided by the red glow in the sky.

Dawn came suddenly, and I noticed the black cloud over Dunkirk was now much closer. I was so exhausted I had to sit down for a rest. I opened the tin of corned beef and packet of biscuits, and after eating them I decided to move on again – I knew that if I sat too long my legs would become stiff. Later, when the black cloud of smoke seemed very close and I could see the silhouettes of buildings in the distance, I knew my journey was nearly over and staggered on with fresh hope.

Half an hour later I found myself on the coast road looking out over the English Channel. I collapsed on the sand dunes which overlooked the beach – there were troops everywhere – some sitting down, some wandering aimlessly about. All the time more men were climbing over the dunes and joining them.

I heard the sound of aircraft approaching – two dark shapes passed overhead, flying low over the beach. Seconds later the chatter of their machine guns echoed across the sands. I watched in horror as the men ran around panic stricken, trying to find shelter from the hail of lead that was pouring down on them from the sky. I saw bodies falling face down in the sand – laying still in grotesque positions. A few brave souls raised their rifles and fired at the aircraft, with very little hope of hitting them. The planes made two sweeps over the beach, then passed low over where I lay in the sand-dune. I could clearly see the dark shapes of the pilots, huddled in their cock-pits, the black crosses on the wings and fuselage then they were gone. Silence reigned for a few seconds, then the beach became alive with men again. There were cries for the 'medics' to attend the wounded and dying.

It was at this time I noticed the little ships approaching from the sea. They came in as close as they dare to the shore, waiting for the lines of men who had started to wade out in the water towards them. They clambered on board one by one, and as each ship became full, it pulled away and headed out to sea.

It was a motley fleet – small launches, pleasure boats, fishing boats, in fact, craft of all shapes and sizes. I marvelled at the sight –

183

the organisation, the patience and calmness of the men as they waited their turn. Nobody tried to jump the queue. The terrifying scream of a diving Stuka dive bomber filled the air, the crowded beach was under attack once more. Three of these aircraft screeched down and swooped low, raining death and destruction on the waiting men and boats. I saw the bombs leave the planes – saw the clouds of sand, mingled with human bodies and flung into the air as they exploded. One small boat, loaded with men, received a direct hit as it pulled away from the shore. Seconds later, the sea was littered with pieces of timber and human remains. This was the first time in my life I had witnessed a carnage of this nature – I felt sick!

The attack had only lasted about five minutes – as they left, one of the aircraft flew in my direction. I watched in horror as a small black object left the plane and fell towards me. My heart pounding, I crouched low in a dune, trying to bury my head in the sand – not even thinking about my other end being exposed! I waited. I heard the loud whine before the bomb exploded – about ten yards away. The ground shook – there was a rush of air, then pieces of shrapnel whined over my head. A shower of sand descended on me, then the plane was gone, leaving a dead silence – I quickly realised how lucky I had been!

Eventually, I got to my feet and shook myself, trying to get rid of the sand. Glancing towards the beach, I saw that once again it was crowded with human beings. The medics were quickly on the scene – trying to separate the dead from the wounded; I didn't envy them their gruesome task.

I sat down again, taking stock of the situation. I looked over to the harbour wall – it was about two hundred yards to my right. The dark shape of a ship showed above the wall, and I could see smoke billowing from its single funnel – was it preparing to move off? I wondered. I knew I had to make a decision – do I join the carnage on the beach, hoping to get away before I'm killed or maimed, or make for the harbour and try to get on the boat. Another air raid quickly made my mind up for me – I chose the harbour!

There was only one ship at the quay; it was a medium-sized merchantman. I saw English and French soldiers climbing a rope net that dropped onto the deck. I ran forward, realising that the ship

184

was beginning to move away from the quay. A six foot gap appeared, and in desperation I jumped across the void, clutching at the net. My rifle slipped off my shoulder and fell into the water – I hung grimly onto the rope netting. Glancing down at the dark waters beneath me, I saw the gap had now widened, I knew there was no turning back. I shuddered; if I lost my grip and fell into that murky blackness, I would drown – I couldn't swim! I took a firmer grip and scrambled up the net. Reaching the top, helping hands pulled me onto the deck, where I was greeted by several British servicemen.

I found out later that it was a Scandinavian registered vessel, and there were about sixty British and an equal number of French soldiers on board.

As the ship left the harbour and headed out into the channel, we were attacked by a dive-bomber, but luckily the bombs fell into the water and we carried on unscathed.

A cheer went up when we sighted the white cliffs of Dover. The ship heaved to about a mile from the shore, and a destroyer approached. Aldis lamps blinked across the water as messages were exchanged. The destroyer left and we were soon on our way – but not towards Dover! To our consternation, the ship turned and headed out into the channel, and the white cliffs soon disappeared.

"Perhaps they're taking us to Southampton." Somebody said. Our spirits rose – 'Southampton, of course, that's it!'

Night came and we huddled together on the deck trying to sleep. I awoke suddenly, realising the ships engines had stopped. A light glow in the sky heralded dawn as I peered over the side of the ship. We had anchored off-shore, close to a harbour entrance. I aroused my companions, and they quickly crowded to the side of the ship.

"That looks like Cherbourg!" somebody exclaimed, "I came here often in peacetime."

"Cherbourg." The name echoed along the deck.

"But it can't be – " a lone voice offered.

But it was Cherbourg – we had been taken back to France!

The consternation must have shown on our faces when we landed on the quay-side, to be met by a British officer.

"I am sorry about this, chaps," he said "we'll get you back to England as soon as possible."

185

"But why have we been bought back to France?" He was asked.

"You were on a foreign ship. The British authorities wouldn't allow it to dock in England."

"But they must have known there were British troops on board." Somebody argued.

The officer looked embarrassed. "I am sorry chaps – but that's all I know!"

"Bloody red tape!" Came the reply – expressing all our sentiments.

We watched as the French troops were led away, then we were taken by truck to a barrack building, where we were given food and drink. Three days later a small paddle steamer arrived in the harbour – our transport back to England."

I have tried to find out the name of the paddle steamer that took Arthur back to England – but with no 'real' success. I wondered whether it could have been the *Medway Queen* which carried on rescuing troops throughout Operation Dynamo.

One other person who was helped by the *Medway Queen* and who arrived back on June 2nd, was Albert Powell. He was a lorry driver in The Royal Signals, attached to 3 Corps Medium Artillery H.Q. He writes:

"On the retreat from Belgium, we got to Poperinghe on the 24th May. Whilst there, we were heavily dive-bombed and lost our commanding officer. We then started to drive towards Bergues, but before arriving there we were stopped at a cross roads by military police and told to make for Dunkirk instead. A bit further along the road we were stopped again and told to dump the lorry; then to proceed on foot.

By this time our unit was gradually getting split up – things were chaotic. By the time we got to the beaches there were only four of us in our group. We huddled together in the sand-dunes for protection from constant bombing and machine gunning. The bombing was ineffectual – just blowing up loads of sand, but the machine gunning was a different matter. To complete this nightmare scene, there was smoke coming from the oil tanks on fire at Dunkirk. At dawn the next day we were marshalled in groups of fifty by an officer or senior N.C.O, and marched down to the waters edge, where discipline was maintained by a naval beachmaster. Each group was called in turn –

woe betide anyone who stepped out of line and tried to go out of turn! I saw one group run out of line and the person in charge was promptly shot by the beachmaster.

Owing to the shallow draft of the beach, the first job was getting on to a rowing boat which took us a little way out, and where we were transferred to a launch which then took us to the larger vessels laying further off. On the way to the bigger ships, our launch was bombed, and although we didn't suffer a direct hit, one bomb hit the water close enough to us to swamp the boat and I found myself in the water; luckily I could swim. Having divested myself of my pack etc. I surfaced and looked around and saw that there was a ship closer to me than the shore, so I struck out for her. She was a converted minesweeper called the *Medway Queen*. I was hauled out of the water totally exhausted – so were my mates.

Before long, the old paddle steamer was on her way, and we soon arrived at Ramsgate. I remember it was a fine day and very warm, and by the time we got there my clothing had practically dried on me. After a smashing welcome from the W.V.S. we got on a train which took us to Devizes – we were billeted in a gymnasium. In the middle of the night, for some unknown reason, we were given a medical inspection, we must have been a funny sight standing there naked – before collapsing back onto our mattresses. We were eventually returned to our units.

As a sequel to all this, whilst on holiday with my family in 1958 on The Isle of Wight, imagine my surprise when I came across the *Medway Queen* anchored on the Medina river, being used as a floating restaurant. Unfortunately it was closed, so we couldn't go aboard. Now, shamefully, she is a rotting hulk lying at a berth in the Medway; I hope her luck soon changes – she deserves the recognition just as much as the *Cutty Sark* or the *Mary Rose*, like them, she is part of the history of this country – a ship to be proud of!"

Among the rearguard troops arriving on the beaches at this time was Harry Stanley, a regular in The Royal Engineers. He had just come out of The Military College of Science as an artificer; before this he had served as an apprentice for five years at Woolwich – engineering was his vocation. The job that the Royal Engineers wanted him to do was to keep the guns firing. He had had his first baptism of firing the big guns at the age of twenty, in 1939, when stationed in Scotland. His first job though, on the declaration of war, was getting all the vehicles camouflaged – this included many civilian vehicles taken on by the army.

On September 24th 1939, they took everything with them when they left Southampton for Brest. When the Blitzkrieg started on May 10th they were sent into Belgium. By May 16th, with the retreat in full swing, they started fighting rearguard actions – including giving covering fire for The Grenadier Guards whilst they retreated from one of the forward positions. They carried on fighting rearguard actions through Poperinghe and Lille . It was near Lille that Harry was given the heartbreaking job of blowing up their guns – "One up the spout, one up the breech!"

After this they drove towards Dunkirk, but when they were about thirty miles away they had to leave their transport in a field, that too was destroyed. They then fought rearguard actions all the way to the coast – the last of these actions, at La Panne. They didn't leave the beaches here until June 2nd, by which time navy patrol vessels were looking out especially for those who had been fighting rearguard actions. Harry told me that although there were still a few hundred men left on the beaches, it was nothing like the mass of troops he had seen on first arriving there. I asked him if he was frustrated at seeing all those men being rescued knowing he had to stay until the end – or nearly to the end. He replied, "No, not at all – I was only 20 years of age at that time of course, and it was the excitement I wanted!"

He was eventually taken off the beaches on June 2nd by a naval patrol boat and taken to *H.M.S. Codrington*, which eventually took him to Dover. During his time on the beaches he had been wounded in one of his arms; this was attended to at Dover and later at a cottage hospital at Wimbourne in Dorset.

Back on the home shores, with the evacuations from Dunkirk now getting near to conclusion, there were more French troops arriving all the time at the ports around the south and south east coast. When the British troops arrived, they were immediately given postcards or telegram forms to fill in to let loved ones know that they were alright, and safely back from across the channel. With the French troops, this was more difficult. They could still write home, but with the strict censorship now imposed, there was a problem, and Admiral Ramsay was aware of this. Accordingly, he approached one of his staff at Dover, Florence Fullager, for help in this matter. Her grandson, Robert Chown, on seeing in his local paper that I needed as many 'first hand' accounts that I could get for writing this book, has written the following to me:

"My grandmother, Florence Fullager (Nana) of Folkestone, was trained by the Red Cross at the Royal Victoria hospital, Folkestone. As the situation deteriorated in May 1940, she was told to report to The Royal Victoria immediately, even though she had not received her uniform yet. She was sent straight to the Buckland Hospital, Dover, and remained there as a resident in the nurses home.

My grandmother spoke fluent French, having been born to English parents living in Chantilly – she was brought up there. As the French soldiers were now arriving more frequently, she was asked personally by Admiral Ramsay to write letters to loved ones for the ones that were more seriously wounded. In spite of the fact that many of these were extremely seriously wounded and not expected to live, she wrote that they were safe and might soon be home – if they so requested. Many of these French soldiers were middle age reservists.

One day, after being given some leave, Nana was sitting under a railway bridge waiting for a bus to go back to Folkestone. She was writing in her notebook in a mixture of English and French. A young soldier considered she was acting suspiciously in a restricted area, and asked to see her identity card. She didn't carry it with her – she considered such things unimportant! The soldier took away her notebook and arrested her. He hailed the bus and escorted her to Folkestone police station. Once they got there, she was instantly recognised by one of the policemen on duty. She was well known locally as her husband had been chairman of the Chamber of Commerce and also the general manager of Lewis and Hyland's department store near the police station.

Amongst the people who were making up the crews of the 'little ships' going to the beaches at Dunkirk at this time, the ages ranged from the early twenties upwards. I have already written about

189

Commander Lightoller aboard *Sundowner* – he was sixty six at the time. A man From Deal, who took an active part on *Golden Spray II*, was a sprightly seventy. But going to the other end of the scale and aboard one of the *Sun* tugs was a young man whose mother had expected him home for tea one afternoon, but didn't see him again for two weeks – during which time he was one of the crew aboard *Sun XII* at Dunkirk. His name is Albert Barnes, and at that time in 1940 when he went on his adventure, he had just left school, and was fourteen and a half years of age.

Albert told me that he remembers going to and fro to the beaches; it seemed as though they were going at it non stop. He spent most of his time as general 'dogsbody' – making cups of tea, washing up and other such tasks. He also remembers that when they got back to Dover he noticed some men on one of the ships coming in had their legs hanging over the gunwales, they looked dog tired, and could even have been asleep. As they came to berth against the quayside, there were screams as their legs were crushed – there was nothing anyone could do – it all happened so quickly.

When he did eventually get home, he told his astonished mother and other relatives where he had been – it was the first they knew of it! He was so tired, that after sitting down he flaked out completely. They had to undress him, wash him and put him to bed; this was after having quite a job in extricating him from his boots. They also had difficulty in getting his socks off, but when they did at last manage to – they stood up like Wellington boots!

On June 2nd, Captain Tennant signalled Admiral Ramsay at Dover, that the evacuation was complete, but there were still ships carrying on, including some of the smaller craft, and they would carry on during the early hours of the next day and the following night as well. One of these was another one of the *Sun* tugs – *Sun XV*. There was also the *Abdy Beauclerk* – the Aldburgh lifeboat, and, as well as these, there were the final rearguard troops, as well as a large number of French troops who had formed the main body of the rearguard and were still arriving on the beaches and in the harbour.

Chapter Twelve

Late Arrivals – Last Departures

E arly in the morning of Sunday June 2nd, a chaplain of the
British Expeditionary Force celebrated Holy Communion
in the Dunkirk dunes. He might well have offered up a prayer of
thanks for the successful evacuation of a huge amount of men from
the Dunkirk area during the whole operation – certainly, the day
before, Saturday June 1st had been a memorable day during
Operation Dynamo.

Jim Hague of The Grenadier Guards was another of the late
arrivals on the beaches, having been involved in some of the
critical rearguard actions. His army service had begun in 1938
after walking into an army recruiting office in Sheffield and
enlisting in the Grenadiers. He spent several months training at
Caterham Barracks – hard training! He passed out in December
1938 and joined the Kings Company of the Grenadier Guards,
stationed at Chelsea Barracks. He had only had ten months to
proudly wear the scarlet tunic and bearskin when war was
declared, and he had to hand this in exchange for regulation
khaki.

He had later enjoyed crossing the channel to Cherbourg – it had
all the makings of an exciting new adventure for this nineteen year
old Yorkshire lad. The date they crossed the channel was September
30th 1939. The winter of 39/40 was one of the worst on record at
that time – "Just terrible!" Jim said. "I shall never forget it, the
ground was frozen so solid it was like iron – even the pick-axes
broke on impact with the ground whilst we were digging trenches
near the French/Belgian border. The coldness was beyond
description, but it was considered 'un-Guardsman like' to turn up

191

our coat collars or wear the mittens that had been sent to us from home, to keep out the bitter winds."

Later, on May 11th – with the Blitzkrieg in full swing, the battalion moved to Louvain, but it was at this time that the 7th Guards Brigade, part of Montgomery's 3rd. Brigade, were ordered to retreat – first back to Brussels, and then to a village called Furnes, not far from the coast, where they fought a long rearguard action while the evacuation of Dunkirk was in progress.

After this, whilst they were making their own way to be rescued, they were consistently attacked by enemy aircraft.

"It was a terrible sight," Jim said, "there were refugees everywhere on the roads – and dead bodies all over the place. I remember passing a tram full of dead people; it was a total nightmare!"

They were ordered to make for Bray-Dunes, but by the time they got there they were told that there would be no more pick-ups from that point, and that they would have to walk along the beaches to Dunkirk – about another ten miles of hard walking! It was June 1st and the Germans were closing in on all sides by this time – the defence perimeter now being even closer to the beaches. There were still thousands of soldiers waiting to be picked up, and the Luftwaffe were relentless in the consistency of their horrific attacks on targets that could only answer back with a shot from a rifle, or short burst from a Bren-gun. Many were just being mown down – it was utter chaos!

When the little ships came into shore there was a mad scramble to get on them, causing some of them to sink with the weight. Jim actually saw one man get shot for trying to get onto an overloaded boat – it was that bad! He spent over twenty four hours on the beaches, until he and a friend were picked up by a small rowing boat and taken to a minesweeper, which eventually took them to Dover. They arrived there on June 3rd.

At this time, although there were still some British troops being picked up at Dunkirk, the French troops were now arriving in even larger numbers. Some of these would be picked up – but unfortunately, many of them would be left behind.

One of the boats that was picking up both British and French troops was the Aldeburgh lifeboat *Abdy Beauclerk*. There were two

192

lifeboats at Aldeburgh at the time of Dunkirk – the number two boat, the *Lucy Lavers*, had only arrived there on May 17th. She was a self-righter driven by a single 35h.p petrol Weyburn engine, giving a top speed of seven knots. Both these boats were duly taken across from Dover. Not much is known about the *Lucy Lavers* at Dunkirk, but thanks to the naval officer in charge of the *Abdy Beauclerk*, Lt. Charles Strudwick, it is known that this lifeboat was responsible for picking up hundreds of troops from the beaches, and taking them out to the awaiting ships on the last days of the operation, and that on their last trips they mainly picked up French troops.

One particularly heartening story, thanks to the initiative shown by several of the French troops, concerns the Thames pleasure cruiser, *Tigris I*. In chapter seven I told of the Hastings brothers being ordered to break up the engine on *Tigris I* and abandon her. It was thought that this was the last of her, but some of the French troops came across her and decided that although the engine was no good, if they could plug the holes they might be able to, somehow, get her across the channel. They duly plugged the holes, and in desperation to get away from the Germans, who at that time were quite close to the beaches, they managed to re-float her. They also managed to get her to as far as the Goodwin Sands, where a naval tug found her laying 'crippled' and towed her into Ramsgate Harbour.

Still on the beaches on June 2nd, were the naval shore party that included Victor Chanter. In continuing his correspondence to me (see chapter 3) Vic writes "Soon, with the evacuation of the gun crews along the beach, it would be time for the demolition of everything of use to the enemy. I suppose it could have been regarded as a vandals' training ground – devastation strewn over miles of sand.

As the numbers awaiting evacuation dwindled, and the chances of being left behind increased, our officer began letting our group off one at a time along with the army. With night-time drawing in on what was to be our last day, just in case things went wrong, we spent quite a bit of our time searching for suitable floating material for ourselves.

During the darkness later that evening, whilst the officer and I were helping some of the remaining soldiers into a boat from what was left of our makeshift pier of lorries, he asked who I was and suggested I should leave with the next lot. An hour or so later we

193

came together again and, discovering who I was, said, 'I thought I told you to go off with the last boat.' I remember making some weak remark 'that my services might be required for getting the last boats away, as the tide was going out.' We knew it was time to leave when we could see the flash of gunfire behind us in the town, and shrapnel was hissing in the water all around us.

But where was our transport? We made up a group of four and wondered along the beach to find two dinghies we had previously earmarked. These we carried to the waters edge, and once again we heard the disturbing hiss of shrapnel, which hadn't been noticeable on the sand. We waded out until we were able to pull ourselves into the boats. The officer and I were together in one (perhaps this time he was taking no chances with me), and his orders were that both dinghies should stay as close as possible, as we paddled into the darkness. How far we went out with the receding tide, I've no idea, but out of the blackness a voice hailed us and we came alongside – scrambling nets were already down the ships sides.

A voice rasped "Up you go." My immediate reply was, "After you, sir." The officer, by now a little confused at my well meant but unseamanlike manner, shouted a brisk, "Get aboard!" I was back in the Royal Navy.

Well almost. Grabbing at the ropes of the scrambling net was the first thing we had done, and no way were we going to release our hold until we were on the rescue vessel. My next job was to stand, usually fairly hazardous in a tiny dinghy in a swell but not in these circumstances. I pulled myself upright and hauled my legs over to the rope rungs. At this point I should explain to the layman a disquieting phenomenon. As a person's foot steps onto the rope of the netting, with that person's full weight, any adjacent rungs tighten to the horizontal as the rung taking the weight drops to its lowest point. (Are you still with me?) The next step taken has the same effect, and so on. One has the feeling of taking gigantic steps upwards and getting nowhere. That being understood, I was getting nowhere; my arms were pulling me up but me feet suddenly become lead weights, the legs were unable to raise them to the next rung. Welcoming hands reached down and hauled me aboard. The officer suffered the same indignity with the same gratitude.

There was no feeling of a job well done. No, it was all in a weeks work. Something required doing and it got done, and I remember amongst others on top deck, I just 'got my head down.'

Upon arrival in England, I joined seething streams of servicemen on railway stations and trains with ant-like purpose of rejoining their units. Eventually I arrived at Chatham R.N. Barracks to discover that from the uniform I had changed into on La Panne beach, I had contracted scabies. What followed was a process of kit fumigation and/or burning. The infected parts of my body had to be scrubbed to break open the skin in order to treat the parasitic mites. Ugh! But I was one of the lucky ones.

After a stay in hospital quarantine, leave was very welcome."

The one but last narrative in this book, comes from a member of the British Expeditionary Force who wasn't taken from the jetty at Dunkirk Harbour until the early hours of June the fourth. He is Bob Pendleton, Military Medal. Royal Corps of Signals. 'L' Section. 139 Infantry Brigade. 46th Division.

Bob, from Nottingham, after arriving in France had later had to escort a convoy into Belgium, he says:

"We had orders to blow up a munitions factory in Lesquin in Belgium. After this was done, I was given the job of looking after a brigadier and taking him back to H.Q. I had been ordered to ensure his safety, his name was Brigadier Chichester Constable, he was from Hull – he was a grand chap."

During this time, Bob, on a motor cycle, was being sent to various places delivering messages, after which he would return to his unit and the Brigadier each time. On one of his journeys he had to go to Bergues, about ten miles from Dunkirk; this town Bob describes as being very much like York – surrounded by a wall and a river. The only entrances were wooden bridges over the moat. The town was completely surrounded by vehicles – most of them on fire! The town was deserted and he had to leave his motor cycle after he had crossed the bridge. He then had to find his way down to the Town Hall, in thick smoke, and in order to breathe more easily, he soaked a towel in the moat and held it over his nose and mouth. When he got to the Town Hall he had to tell some troops that were still there to make their way to Dunkirk immediately.

195

On returning to the bridge, he discovered his motor cycle had been stolen, but after a brief search of the area, he came across another one and rode this one back to the Brigadier.

Another message he was told to deliver, was to a farm held by the 2/5th Foresters. When he arrived there the farm was deserted, so after delivering some other messages, he returned to the Brigadier again. Bob says, "The Brigadier asked me to go back and try just one more time at the farm, but when I arrived there I nearly ran into the advance patrol of the German army – motor cycles and side cars with machine guns mounted on them. My bike did a quick u-turn and I went for it, hoping that the Jerry's weren't following. I got back to the Brigadier without much trouble and informed him that the farm was occupied by the Germans. He said 'Right, let's go to Dunkirk – straight away!' When we got there we saw some fishing smacks coming into the harbour – it was 6am on the fourth of June. We went straight to the jetty. We had to put a twelve foot plank across a part of it that had been blown away. I remember I made about ten journeys over this plank taking as many men as I could. We then climbed down the side of the jetty and into the fishing smacks – the crews of these boats all helping us. As we pulled away out of the harbour the Stukas came over, but for some reason refrained from attacking us, and flew away.

We landed at Ramsgate where we were given a lovely reception; with the ladies of various voluntary organisations handing out to us much needed and appreciated refreshments."

With the Germans now so close at hand, and time fast running out for those left in Dunkirk or still arriving there, I feel that this would be the right place to put the final narrative of all those sent to me – a story of three more 'little ships' – the Thames tugs *Sun IV* and *Sun XV* and also the hospital ship *Paris*. In the following narrative by the master of the tug *Sun XV* – there is an account about the desperate but unsuccessful search for survivors from the fast sinking hospital ship *Paris*. From 1934, up to the outbreak of war, the *Paris* had become a familiar sight to the people of Brighton – frequently sailing from the Palace Pier – and, in a way, taking over from where the *Brighton Belle* had left off from to take up duties in the Bristol Channel. She was another ship well known to my parents and grandparents – along with the *Brighton Belle*. In the First

196

World War she had operated as a minelayer She had been converted as a hospital ship in January 1940, and was at Calais before Operation Dynamo had begun. The *Paris* had arrived at Dunkirk on May 25th, along with another converted hospital ship, the *Isle of Thanet*. For several days the *Paris* had taken on board large numbers of wounded troops, and made several crossings, including ones to Newhaven, which she was entirely familiar with because her old run used to be from Newhaven to Brighton Palace Pier and then to Dieppe. On the way back, in those days, they missed Brighton out and went direct from Dieppe to Newhaven. The charge for the trip was 12/6p – allowing five hours ashore in France. Sadly though, on June 2nd 1940 she had been bombed and sunk.

Here is the account made by the master of *Sun XV* – J.J. Belton:

"On Thursday May 30th 1940, we were instructed to go to the Tilbury landing stage for de-magnetising, as we were going to Dunkirk to assist in bringing the B.E.F. back to England – at midnight we were prepared to leave.

On instructions from the S.N.O. Tilbury, we took in tow twelve life boats and proceeded to Southend – where we would receive further instructions. On arrival at Southend we received further instructions to proceed to Ramsgate. Later on, at 2.30 p.m. we received orders from the S.N.O. at Ramsgate to proceed to Dunkirk – taking six of the lifeboats in tow. On approaching the Dunkirk roads, we were attacked by a large group of German bombers; although the bombs fell close by there were no direct hits and no casualties.

At 10.15 p.m. on the 31st we received orders from one of H.M. destroyers, to proceed a further four miles eastwards of Dunkirk. When there, we were ordered to proceed a further six miles to the beaches at La Panne, where we were to use the lifeboats we were towing for collecting troops off the beaches. We anchored there at midnight. At 12.15 a.m. on June 1st our boats left for the beach – approx. fifty yards from where we had anchored. The German artillery was relentless, there were shells landing all around us. In these very bad circumstances our crews managed to ferry between 70 and 80 soldiers aboard *Sun XV*, but we lost all our boats.

At 2 a.m. we hove up anchor and proceeded down the roads at slow speed – we were continuously machine-gunned, but with skilful management we made the open channel without harm and proceeded on our way to Ramsgate.

At 4.30am, in a position 3 miles westerly of the Ruytengin Buoy, we spoke to two government vessels – X149 a Sheerness Dockyard Lighter (later reported sunk) and YC72 a Chatham Dockyard Lighter. Both of these were disabled with engine trouble, and a lieutenant asked us to tow them to Ramsgate – it was too dangerous for them to be laying where they were because of attacks from the Luftwaffe. We took them in tow and anchored off Ramsgate at 9 a.m. Small motor craft from Ramsgate disembarked the troops.

On June 2nd at 9 p.m., we were boarded by a naval commander and instructed to proceed to the aid of the hospital ship *Paris* which had been bombed and was in immediate need of help. We sighted the *Paris* at 11.11 p.m. and encircled the ship, which had a bad list to starboard. We carried on encircling – trying to find any survivors, but we found no-one. We managed to get our wire made fast to the ships starboard quarter, but the wire parted at exactly the same time as we were again attacked and heavily machine gunned. It was too dangerous to attempt salvage. We steamed around for several hours, until at 3.40 a.m. we sighted the drifter *Yorkshire Lass*, disabled with engine trouble and loaded with troops – we took her in tow. At 4.37 a.m. the drifter made a signal to us that the engines had been repaired and we gave orders for the tow-rope to be let go. We then proceeded to Ramsgate where we anchored at 7.45 a.m. This was on Monday 3rd June.

At 11.20 a.m. we received orders to proceed into Ramsgate Harbour to take on sand bags for the protection of those on board.

Whilst anchored outside Ramsgate, at 1.20 p.m. we received instructions that at 5.00 p.m. we were to proceed to Dunkirk for the final embarkation. At 10.35 p.m., having only had slight delays on crossing, by mines which the enemy had laid, we commenced to embark troops – using the four boats we were towing. At 2 a.m. June 4th we entered the pier heads and went along the eastern arm of Dunkirk Harbour, but found practically all had been embarked, and at 2.30 a.m. we left the pier-heads and proceeded on our crossing to Ramsgate. At 3.20 a.m. whilst steaming at full speed because of the fast approaching light of dawn, we were attacked and machine

198

gunned by German aircraft again – but without casualties. At 4.20 a.m. we took in tow a drifter that had developed engine trouble and took her into Ramsgate and anchored at 8.15 a.m.

At 10.00 a.m. we received orders to tow the scoot *Reiger* from Ramsgate to Tilbury where we arrived at 7.50 p.m."

In addition to this account, also signed by J.J.Belton, he says that on returning to Ramsgate, after unsuccessfully trying to find survivors from the *Paris*, they had run aground on the approach to Ramsgate and had had to be towed off by another of the *Sun* tugs – *Sun IV*.

The report from *Sun IV* on June 3rd says that they towed *Sun XV* off at 7 a.m. Another report from *Sun IV* dated June 4th says that they assisted the destroyer *Malcolm*, which was the last destroyer to load up with troops – this was to keep her alongside the mole until she had moored.

It would appear from this report and other reports, that although the *Malcolm* had been the last destroyer to load up, she wasn't the last one to leave – that dangerous honour fell to the *Shikari*.

H.M.S. *Malcolm* had been ordered to go over again by Admiral Ramsay, after he had learned that although the British troops had been evacuated, there were still thousands of French troops hoping to be 'lifted' across the channel.

The last destroyers on the scene were the *Express*, the *Malcolm* and the *Shikari*. H.M.S *Shikari* had gone out by way of route Z on the evening of the 3rd of June. Owing to the failure the previous night of the blocking of Dunkirk Harbour, it was decided to have another try. The ships used in the blocking operation were the *Shikari* and the two speedboats *MTB 107* and *MA/SB 10*, and for the actual blocking the mvs, *Gourko* – 1,975 tons, the *Moyle*, 1,761 tons and the *Pacifico* 687 tons.

At 02.30hrs. on the 4th June, Captain Dangerfield on board *MA/SB 10* led the ships to the entrance to the harbour. The *Gourko* hit a magnetic mine and sank near the entrance to the harbour. The survivors were picked up by *MA/SB 10* and ferried to the *Shikari* and taken aboard. The *Pacifico* was scuttled where the *Gourko* should have gone, and the *Moyle* rammed the inner western pier, next to another sunken ship the *Westcove*.

At 03.30 hours, shelling recommenced, causing many casualties and making further visits by the destroyers out of the question.

Under heavy fire, H.M.S. *Shikari* paid a final brief visit to the eastern mole, she was the last destroyer to leave the scene – she had over 300 French troops on her when she left.

As dawn was breaking, Lieutenant Cameron, on board *MTB 107*, decided to have one last look around the harbour. He could see thousands of French troops left standing on the mole and the pierheads but the position had now become hopeless – he turned *MTB 107* around and headed for home – she was the last boat to leave the harbour.

Back at home, mother had had word that her brother Jimmy was back – unscathed and soon to come home on leave. Later, he told us he had been extremely lucky – unlike so many friends, "Now not with us any more." Apart from this, he simply didn't like talking about all that had taken place.

My Uncle Nat, a Lt. Cmdr. at the end of the war, also didn't talk much about his experiences at first, but later, he did relate some of what happened to my father when they went on fishing expeditions together – it is a pity that neither of them put pen to paper and wrote their accounts of those times down; what I remember of the stories told are too 'patchy' to attempt to write them here.

Dunkirk had prepared us for the Battle of Britain that would soon be being fought in the clear blue skies above us – a defeat had been turned into a victory and had brought us together as a people. We still feared being invaded – this remained a live threat for quite some time, but we lived with that and other fears. Thanks to the 'never say die' spirit which was instilled in us by the rescue of over a third of a million human beings, we were able "To fight another day," and eventually secure the victory.

After Dunkirk, peoples attitudes changed. My father found himself having lengthy conversations with people, who in previous years, he had only been on nodding terms with. Friendships blossomed and our souls had found a special richness in – "All being in the same boat together."

Epilogue

I have already put all the names of those who contacted me in the acknowledgments, but in tying up a few loose ends in the epilogue I shall mention just a few of them again, in telling what happened to them afterwards. I have also written about what happened to some of 'the little ships'.

Jim Peall, who now lives in Margate, spent five years as a prisoner of war. He was at Stalag 20A at Thorn (now Torun) in Poland. Later he went to Stalag 357 at Fallingbostal, but towards the end of the war, when they could hear the Russian guns in the distance, they were moved again. He spent the last two weeks before repatriation on a sort of walkabout – still under German supervision. Jim told me he soon got fed up with this and one day when they were near a Red Cross post for the wounded, he gave his guards the slip and posed as one of the wounded until eventually being freed by the British Army a few days later.

Vic Knight, also spent five years as prisoner of war. I wrote about him in chapter two – 'The Defence of Calais.' He survived the 'Death March' into Poland, and spent a long time at the largest prisoner of war camp in Poland (Stammlagen). From there he went out on working parties – building roads and such jobs.

Towards the end of the war he took part in a second 'Death March' – this started when the Russian guns could be heard in the distance and the Germans decided to move everyone in the general direction of Germany. This time though, Vic decided enough was enough and escaped whilst on the march. He spent quite some time

201

walking across country, sleeping rough and obtaining what little food he could find from farms and various other places on the way. After a time he crossed the border into Czechoslovakia – eventually to be repatriated.

Joe Nixon spent three months in hospital at Epsom, after coming home in a hospital ship from Calais (Chapter 2). During a period of convalescence he was attached to the holding battalion of the Coldstream Guards at Regents Park – he spent some of this time 'plane spotting' from a nearby roof. Later, he fought in the desert campaign – his last action was at Mount Ornito, at the time of the Battle for Cassino. It was here that the original Dunkirk No 1 Company (Joe's Company) of the 2nd. Battalion Coldstream Guards, got a 'bloody nose,' and was so decimated that for several months of the campaign it was taken over by S Company of the Scots Guards.

After the war, Joe joined the Metropolitan police, and had a very colourful career whilst stationed in the Notting Hill area – a book has been written about him called, 'Nick of Notting Hill' – it is written by Anthony Richardson.

Joe spent eleven years in the police force before resigning and eventually joining, what was then called, The Prison Probation Service.

When it became known to the Falmouth family (Lord Falmouth) that Guardsman Joe Nixon had been with their son just before he was so tragically killed on that dark night in 1940, Lady Falmouth visited Joe in hospital at Epsom. During that visit Joe gave her Lieutenant Boscawen's small silver Coldstream Capstar. Lieutenant Colonel H.G.R. Boscawen – nephew to Lt. Evelyn Boscawen has proudly worn this capstar since he was commissioned into the Coldstream Guards in 1976.

In May 1990, Joe Nixon and his brother Jim, also a former Coldstream Guardsman, were invited by Lord Falmouth to join the Boscawen family at the dedication of the headstone to Lieutenant the Hon. Evelyn Boscawen. With the help of the Commonwealth War Graves Commission the family had recently managed to trace the grave of Lt. Boscawen, who had an 'Unknown Lieutenant' headstone, and fifty years after his death, held a service of dedication

202

in the towns cemetery at Pecq, near Lille. Bishop David Say, close friend of Evelyn Boscawen, conducted the service; Bishop Say's wife had met Joe through the prison service in Maidstone, and put him back in touch with the Boscawens.'

Joe, a very active member of the Dunkirk Veterans Association now lives with his wife in Maidstone – we quite often have enjoyable conversations on the telephone.

Frank Brookshaw, who wrote to me with his excellent account of life aboard one of the destroyers at the time of Dunkirk – *H.M.S. Anthony* – is well and active. I shall never forget that when I admired a framed picture on one of the walls of his sitting room at his home in Brighton, he immediately took it down and handed it to me after I had said I'd like a copy of it for this book. It's now safely back on his wall – I'm glad to say.

Steve Hastings, a relative of Harry Hastings, the landlord of the Gloucester Arms at Kingston at the time of Dunkirk, who also owned the Thames pleasure boat *Tigris I* is putting the finishing touches to a book he has written about the adventures of this boat.

He has written this as a complete adventure story – a good idea, taking into consideration all that happened to *Tigris I* – before, during and after the evacuation – which is a lot more than I have written about in this book. The title will be 'Little Heroes' – he hopes it will be ready for publication soon.

Naiad Errant, the motor yacht taken to Dunkirk by Able Seaman Palmer is at present having an overhaul at a boatyard on the River Medway – she is the pride and joy of her owners, Sandy Evans and John Richards. Sandy Evans, after losing an opportunity to purchase her when she was lying on the river Hamble in 1946, and then losing touch with where she was, spent seven years searching for her. Eventually, he was informed that she was at Southampton – and for sale. He bought her!

John Richards lives near to Sandy Evans on a beautiful stretch of the Thames, and they both hope that *Naiad Errant* will soon have been put right and moored close to them. John is also writing a book about the adventures and time of this lovely boat, and this, of course, will be far more detailed than the brief account of her activities at Dunkirk that I have written about in this book.

The Margate lifeboat, the *Lord Southborough*, after Dunkirk, received the following citation from *H.M.S. Icarus*, and dated 6th June 1940:

Sir,

On behalf of every officer and man in this ship I should like to express to you our unbounded admiration of the magnificent behaviour of the crew of the lifeboat *Lord Southborough* during the recent evacuation from Dunkirk.

The manner in which, with no thought of rest, they brought off load after load of soldiers under continuous shelling, bombing and aerial machine gun fire will be an inspiration to us all as long as we live. We are proud to be the fellow countrymen of such men.

(signed) E.G.Roper. Lieutenant Commander.

The remainder of the war was a very active time for the *Lord Southborough*.

On June 4th 1940, the senior naval officer at Margate said that the boat was required for naval duties. On her first call out with a naval crew, quite a number of things went wrong and it was decided that from then on, whilst still under naval command, she would go out with her own crew. She remained the Margate Lifeboat until 1951 and then served as a reserve boat for the R.N.L.I. until 1955, when she was sold out of service. She is now privately owned – 'alive and well.'

The *Prudential* – the Ramsgate lifeboat at the time of Dunkirk, is also now privately owned and kept by her owner in Suffolk. The East Kent Maritime Trust tried to buy her and bring her to Ramsgate – but without success. The present owner told them that she had become a part of the family and they wouldn't part with the boat for the world.

Later on the trust acquired the yacht *Sundowner*. This was the boat owned by Commander Lightoller, and which one day during the evacuation from Dunkirk, arrived at Ramsgate with 130 troops on

204

board – nearly sinking with the weight. *Sundowner* carried on as a coastal patrol vessel for the remainder of the war. Afterwards, she remained with the Lightoller family for many years. She has now been found a permanent home by The East Kent Maritime Trust, in the harbour at Ramsgate, just near to the East Kent Maritime Museum.

The Shoreham Lifeboat, the *Rosa Woodd and Phyllis Lunn*, served as a lifeboat for thirty years. After her activities at Dunkirk she was involved in a number of rescues in the channel. In November 1941, she was called out to the minesweeper *President Briand*, which was in trouble off Shoreham. Her coxswain was put aboard the *President Briand* to give what assistance he could. Another ship, the *S.S. Goole* went to tow her in, but also got into trouble – the Shoreham lifeboat tried to tow both ships into harbour, but the ropes parted. After going alongside a few times they took off everyone – including their own coxswain. The *Rosa Woodd and Phyllis Lunn* then returned to Shoreham Harbour in treacherous conditions – nearly twelve hours after going out on the call. The acting coxswain, James Upperton, in charge for the first time, earned a silver medal for gallantry. Her motor mechanic, Henry (Harry) Philcox, who I met at the Sussex Yacht Club at Shoreham whilst seeking information for this book, and is now a sprightly ninety years of age, received the Bronze Medal and later the B.E.M.

After the *Rosa Woodd and Phyllis Lunn* was retired from service, she was bought for private use and renamed *Dowager*.

After Dunkirk, the Hastings Lifeboat, – the *Cyril and Lilian Bishop*, had a particularly busy time during The Battle of Britain. In his book, 'The Fishermen of Hastings,' Steve Peak writes – 'The summer and autumn of 1940 saw the most intense air attacks of the war on south east England, and the *Cyril and Lilian Bishop* rescued at least four enemy airmen, shot down in separate incidents. There was considerable hostility towards these fliers, particularly those who had been attacking Hastings. After being pulled out of the sea, one shivering German pilot was given a pullover by a lifeboatman, who also gave him a hefty kick after being given a Nazi salute!

205

After the war, in 1950, she was sold and became a fishing boat. She is now at Simon Evans boatyard at St. Denis-Les-Sens in France. Simon, a lifeboat enthusiast is keen to open a lifeboat museum, and another lifeboat in his care in France at the moment is the *Lucy Lavers* which was the second lifeboat at Aldeburgh.

The tug *Challenge*, which I wrote a little about in chapter nine, after Dunkirk, also served in the first line of our defences against invasion. She helped to tow the Maunsell Towers to the Thames estuary and the Mulberry Harbours to the Normandy beaches for the D-Day landings.

After the war she was owned by four different companies. In 1974 she came to the end of her towing days. Unlike some of the other *Sun* tugs that were eventually broken up, *Challenge* is still with us and in the keen hands of some of the members of the Dunkirk Little Ships Restoration Trust – who bought her in 1993 for the grand sum of £1. These are a group of enthusiasts who give up a lot of their free time in trying to put her to rights; but she also need an urgent financial injection. The following has been written by the Restoration Trust under the heading – A Vision For The Future:

Challenge, when fully restored, has been offered a permanent berth close to the *Cutty Sark* and Sir Francis Chichester's *Gipsy Moth* at Greenwich, where she will be open to the public as a floating Dunkirk Museum, complete with her Oerlikon and Lewis guns. Her lighter will house her visitor centre and permanent exhibition. This will comprise video films and a lecture room. A joint ticketing scheme will provide access to the *Cutty Sark's* 250,000 annual visitors who will help fund the staffing and upkeep.

Challenge will not only provide the public with a permanent memorial to the Evacuation of Dunkirk, but will give enthusiasts an opportunity to see one of the last triple expansion steam engines in full working order, together with five further steam engines providing the ancillary services and displays which will demonstrate the history of London's famous river and the remarkable steam tugs.

But for this vision to become a reality, a sum of £250,000 is urgently required to help the volunteers to complete their work of restoration.

Recently, my youngest son Tim and I motored over to a lonely stretch of the River Medway – not too far from where we live at Rochester. Apart from the tall chimneys of Grain Power Station and various factory buildings dotted about here and there, there are still some isolated places here, and on our journey we saw many healthy looking rabbits scampering along some of the rough tracks that serve as roads. Lying in a creek here is the old paddle steamer the *Medway Queen*. Lying there, in all that isolation – not a soul about apart from us – I wondered why on earth she wasn't perhaps in a 'pride of place' position at Chatham Historic Dockyard as a permanent attraction. Her history certainly deserves such recognition, and having the name Medway in her title should, in a way, entitle her to this stature.

As I write this, I find it a sorry state of affairs that a ship that has given so much pleasure in the past and helped in the saving of thousands of lives at Dunkirk, as well as also having a distinguished war record in the 10th minesweeping flotilla, should now be in danger of being broken up.

Money, of course, is at the root of all the trouble, but one would have thought that the thousands of lives that she saved and deserves to be remembered for, should place her beyond the speculation of the corridors of finance, and preserved as a very special ship in the history of a maritime nation.

To endorse my sentiments on this subject I should like to add the rest of the piece by J.B. Priestley chosen by The Red Cross for their booklet about Dunkirk and printed in 1940 – another part is in chapter four. In this case he was talking about his favourite paddle steamer the *Gracie Fields*, but is of course applicable to all those grand old ladies.

'But now look – this little steamer, like all her brave and battered sisters, is imortal. She'll go sailing proudly down the years in the epic of Dunkirk. And yet our grandchildren, when they learn how we began this war by snatching glory out of defeat, and then swept on to victory, may also learn how the little holiday steamers made an excursion to hell and came back glorious.'

Finally, The Association of Dunkirk Little Ships (A.D.L.S.) and The Dunkirk Little Ships Restoration Trust, continue in their good work, and there are many proud owners of boats that went to Dunkirk – such as the *Sylvia* which I wrote about in chapter nine. She is now a houseboat and home for A.D.L.S. member Ian Pearson and his wife. She is berthed on the Medway and renamed *Wendy Ken*. Her Dunkirk adventures might easily have been forgotten under her new name, had it not been for Lt. Cmdr. Maynard, who was still the harbour master at Ramsgate, and recognised her when she entered the port one day. "I would have recognised her anywhere!" He said, and went on to tell of what he knew of the rescues she had been involved in. Ian and his wife take her across to Dunkirk each year, and will be doing so again this year – the 60th anniversary.

Unfortunately The Dunkirk Veterans Association has now come to the end of a long and memorable road, and the year 2000 marks the last big anniversary of this unique society of 'Brothers' who survived Dunkirk and who permanently remember those that didn't.

Some local societies will carry on in their own areas and still do their own thing, but the feelings will run very deep on this 60th and final anniversary.

They shall grow not old
  as we that are left grow old;
  Age shall not weary them
  nor the years condemn;
  At the going down of the sun
  and in the morning,
  We will remember them.
  When you go home,
  Tell them of us and say
  For your tomorrow
  We gave our today.

Index of Craft

Index of People

The Author

The author with his wife Pamela on a visit to Maytham Hall at Rolvenden in Kent.

This used to be the home of Frances Hodgson Burnett who wrote 'The Secret Garden'.

The Hall was used by Ealing Studios as the headquarters of the British Expeditionary Force in France, in the film – 'Dunkirk'.

David Knowles was born in Brighton and educated at Brighton College Junior School and then – Lancing College.

After serving as a short term regular in the R.A.F. he took up writing as a hobby and eventually more seriously.

Since retiring early from his work in agriculture he has taken up writing full time, and has also started a very small publishing business specialising in the 1940's and in particular World War II.

He is interested in trying to 'keep alive' any stories of that period that deserve to be remembered.